Sweet Paleo

Sweet Paleo

Gluten-Free, Grain-Free Delights

LEA HENDRY VALLE

The Countryman Press
Woodstock, Vermont

Book design and composition by Vicky Vaughn Shea, Ponderosa Pine Design

Published by The Countryman Press, P.O. Box 748, Woodstock, VT 05091
Distributed by W. W. Norton & Company, Inc., 500 Fifth Avenue, New York, NY 10110
Printed in the United States

Photographed by Lea Valle.
Author photo by Gavin Valle.

This book is intended for general informational purposes only, and not as personal medical advice, medical opinion, diagnosis or treatment.

Sweet Paleo
978-1-58157-277-3

10 9 8 7 6 5 4 3

In loving memory of my father, Dr. Durwood Hendry, and to my mother, Louise Hendry Womack, whose love imbued me with an "internal pot of gold" from which I draw strength daily.

Contents

Introduction

My Story

After struggling with persistent health issues for several years, I was convinced that diet was a significant factor. During time spent searching the Internet for news, information and clues about my condition, I became deeply intrigued by one particular word that kept popping up on my computer screen: *Paleo*.

My symptoms had not been eradicated with other ways of eating that were supposedly "healthy," so it was worth a try to see whether Paleo might be right for me. This was more of a total lifestyle change than merely an eating adjustment and I benefited from the total transformation of my eating plan and physical fitness routine. Going Paleo was difficult at first, especially getting through the first days of a thirty-day "elimination diet." But after sticking with it, I experienced rather dramatic results in a fairly short period of time. My energy level increased and my sleep patterns started to improve. Most important, my symptoms began to disappear. After years of seeing various types of medical professionals who tried to determine the root of my health problems and always being told nothing was "wrong" with me, I finally suggested that my doctor test me for celiac disease. When the results came back with a celiac diagnosis, a lot of my prior symptoms suddenly made sense. I had one of those dramatic, *Aha!* moments. Nutrition—my diet—had been making me sick for years. Now that I knew, what should I do about it?

I started my blog, Paleospirit.com, as an answer. It was therapeutic and fun. I have always enjoyed cooking, and I soon developed a love for creating my own unique recipes that conform to my way of eating. It is a challenge but also a joy when I am able to turn a classic dish into something that I and others like me can eat without guilt or fear. Paleo Spirit enables me to share my passions for food, photography and nature in creative ways and, hopefully, help encourage others along the way.

My Philosophy

For some people, food is simply utilitarian. But there are occasions when life demands something more, something special. *Sweet Paleo* is a celebration of foods that add some measure of variety and pleasure to our lives. We join together with friends and family to enjoy meals made for special occasions. Going through life focusing on food merely as fuel, while fine for some, is not for me. I choose to savor those precious moments of human interaction that sometimes include the sharing of special treats.

"I THANK YOU GOD FOR THIS MOST AMAZING DAY, FOR THE LEAPING GREENLY SPIRITS OF TREES, AND FOR THE BLUE DREAM OF SKY AND FOR EVERYTHING WHICH IS NATURAL, WHICH IS INFINITE, WHICH IS YES."
~e.e. cummings~

I believe our daily lives are enhanced in many ways by taking the time to enjoy the beauty of creation. Stop and smell the flowers. Take time to reflect on the beauty that surrounds us. It calms the mind and bolsters the soul. Our enjoyment of food can play a role in this, too. I love when food is not only healthful and delicious, but aesthetically pleasing as well.

What Is Paleo?

Paleo means "older or ancient" and thus the Paleo diet (a.k.a. Paleolithic diet) got its name from the idea that we should be eating the way our preagriculture ancestors ate. Some people place a lot of emphasis on evolutionary science to justify this way of eating. What interests me more, aside from my own positive experience, is the scientific evidence and studies that show eating the foods we were created to eat leads to improved health. We should all think of food as a drug that we are putting into our body multiple times a day. Many of the illnesses plaguing our society, such as heart disease, type 2 diabetes, high blood pressure and cancer, just to name a few, are what are known as diseases of civilization. With that in mind, we should be eating what heals our body and supports our immune and cardiovascular systems and our brain function and keeps our sugar levels stable. The Paleo diet does just that.

WHICH FOODS ARE INCLUDED?

I prefer to think of the Paleo diet as a "way of eating" or "way of life." And what works for one person may not be exactly right for another. However, we can all look forward to improved health if we focus on eating nutrient-dense, noninflammatory, whole foods. You can think of Paleo as more of a "template" that focuses on eating the following foods:

- High-quality sources of protein, such as meat, fowl and seafood
- Lots of colorful, fresh vegetables and fruits
- Healthy fats, such as nuts, seeds, avocados, olive oil and coconut

Eating protein, fresh fruits and vegetables and good fats simply provides much more nutrient density than does theStandard American Diet (SAD), which is high in processed foods. There are tons of amazingly good recipes that use only the above groups of foods along with herbs and spices to keep you from feeling the least bit deprived. Additionally, meals high in protein and good fats tend to lead to a period of satiety that lasts much longer than eating a low-fat, high-carb diet. Thus, you will stay fuller longer and consume fewer calories overall as a result. My personal experience has been that once I shifted my body from primarily sugar and carb burning to fat burning, I am simply not hungry as often. My great epiphany was realizing that I do not have to go around hungry to be fit and lean—and neither do you!

WHICH FOODS ARE EXCLUDED?

The Paleo diet advocates the removal of:

- All grains, including wheat, barley and rye, and even gluten-free grains, such as rice and corn
- Legumes, including soy and peanuts
- Dairy products
- Refined sugar
- Trans fats, hydrogenated oils and other highly processed seed oils
- White potatoes (primarily for individuals with autoimmune disease or those seeking to lose weight)

Some people advocate the elimination of such foods as coffee and alcohol, but I personally find I am able to tolerate consuming these in moderation. For individuals with autoimmune diseases, it may be necessary to go a step further and eliminate certain other foods, such as nuts, eggs and members of the nightshade family (e.g., tomatoes)—at least for a period of time. This is what is generally known as the autoimmune

Paleo protocol. You can learn more about that protocol at www.paleospirit.com or in certain Paleo-focused nutrition books.

> **NOTE:** Dairy is allowed for individuals who have first gone through a period of dairy elimination, followed by a reintroduction of dairy. Anyone who continues to feel well after reintroducing dairy may choose to eat it. This is often referred to as the primal way of eating. If you are able to eat dairy, I suggest you stick to organic, full-fat dairy from grass-fed (pastured) animals, for the best nutrition. A few primal recipes are included in this book, but the vast majority are dairy free or have dairy-free options.

TRY EATING PALEO FOR THIRTY DAYS

It is not as difficult as you think! Lots of good resources for recipes exist in cookbooks and online. See how you feel after thirty days of strict Paleo eating and then reassess. Some people find they can add some limited dairy with no ill effects. Others find they simply feel better continuing on the strict Paleo path.

Paleo as Code Word

Most people, even those who ordinarily follow a healthful diet or even a strict Paleo way of eating, like to have standard treats and desserts from time to time. All things in moderation, right? But for some of us dealing with food sensitivities, intolerances and/or allergies, this simply is not an option. We want to be able to enjoy a piece of pie during the holidays without getting ill. And our children should be able to enjoy birthday cake at a party with their friends.

For me the word *Paleo* is more of a code word for "does not contain the ingredients to which I am allergic or find problematic for my health," rather than mimicking something a caveman would have eaten. Who wants to have to search the Internet for "grain-free, gluten-free, dairy-free, legume-free" this or that, and hope the recipe also uses natural sweeteners? I look for the word *Paleo* because it sums it all up. I know if I find a recipe or cookbook designated as Paleo, it likely conforms to my way of eating. As a responsible adult, I decide how much of a particular food I should or should not eat or serve to my kids. In the case of sweets, it may be in small portions and rare. But when eating a dessert or other treat, I would rather have one that is made of nutrient-dense, highest-possible-quality ingredients than something with empty calories that will make me or my family feel terrible afterward or be detrimental to our health.

Can *Sweet* Ever Be *Paleo*?

You might think "*Sweet Paleo*" is an oxymoron. The practice of using Paleo-approved ingredients to craft foods that are essentially re-creations of modern processed, addictive foods is looked down upon by some people. It is true that our society relies too heavily on processed foods high in carbohydrates, bad fats, preservatives and other problematic ingredients. And it is valid, especially when dealing with a real food addiction, to avoid getting into the habit of making and eating too many recipes that are re-creations of problematic foods. After all, the overconsumption of sugar leads to weight gain, inflammation and blood sugar swings. And the lack of large amounts of processed sugar in a Paleo diet is partly what makes us feel better than we used to. However, in my experience it is far easier to stick to a restricted diet when you know you can have the occasional piece of chocolate cake at a birthday party or pancakes on the weekend. There is nothing wrong with the occasional Paleo baked good or treat, especially if it helps you maintain your eating plan without any major lapses that can damage your health overall.

THE SWEETENERS USED IN *SWEET PALEO*

The sweeteners used in this book are limited to those that are considered unrefined or at least minimally processed compared to refined sweeteners, such as white table sugar. But just because a sweetener is less processed or has more enzymes or minerals, does not mean it is okay to consume it to your heart's content. Humans are hard-wired to love sweet foods, so it is easy to overeat them. Blood sugar imbalances occur after eating too many sweets, even the natural ones! So, it's important to limit even the natural sweets in your diet. And when you do eat sweets, one good way to keep from having a major blood sugar crash is to avoid eating them by themselves. The recipes in this book contain primarily natural, unrefined sugars accompanied by other healthful, nutrient-dense ingredients—such as healthy fats, proteins and fiber. I try to use only as much sweetener as necessary for great flavor, and usually far less than in traditional recipes. Many recipes

lend themselves to adjustments based on your own taste. But be careful. Sometimes my reason for selecting a particular sweetener is simply that it tastes delicious in a particular dish. At other times, it satisfies the needs of the recipe due to such things as texture, color and moisture content and may not be easily substituted. (To learn more about the sweeteners used in this book, see page 16.)

What Is Gluten and Is It Always Bad?

Gluten is a general name for the proteins found in such grains as wheat, barley and rye, among others. Gluten acts as a glue that holds food together. It helps dough rise and maintain its shape. It also gives the final product a chewy texture. Gluten is not necessarily bad. But it is also known to cause adverse health issues, ranging from bloating, gas, diarrhea and vomiting to migraine headaches and joint pain in those who suffer from gluten sensitivity, primarily as a result of celiac disease or nonceliac gluten sensitivity and wheat allergy. Let's take a quick look at what those are:

- **Celiac disease:** The most well-known form of gluten intolerance is celiac disease, which is an inherited autoimmune disorder affecting the digestive process of the small intestine. When people with celiac disease consume gluten, it triggers an immune response that damages their intestines, preventing the absorption of vital nutrients. Even very tiny amounts of gluten can cause an immune response in people with celiac disease. Because gluten can be found in many types of foods, even ones you would not expect, staying completely gluten free is quite difficult. This is one reason why many of us with celiac disease must prepare most, if not all, of our own food.
- **Non-celiac gluten sensitivity:** Also known as gluten intolerance, gluten sensitivity causes the body to mount an immune response when it breaks down gluten during digestion. This is often manifested in gastrointestinal symptoms and can also include such things as fatigue and joint pain, but without incurring damage to the intestines.
- **Wheat allergy** is a classic food allergy in which the immune system responds to a food protein because it considers it dangerous to the body when it is not. Wheat allergy is often marked by skin, respiratory or gastrointestinal reactions to wheat allergens. This immune response usually lasts a short time and does not cause lasting harm to the body.

> **BOTTOM LINE:** Gluten may or may not be a problem for you. Merely eliminating gluten but continuing to eat highly processed foods will never lead to optimal health. The better option is to stick with high-quality, nutrient-dense, non-inflammation-promoting foods and steer clear of anything with processed and unnatural ingredients.

The Problem with Grains, Legumes and Dairy
GRAINS

Although it may run counter to what you have read and heard for years, grains, even the much-touted "healthy whole grains," are not health foods. The Paleo way of eating advocates the elimination of all grains and grain products from the diet. The list of eliminated grains include gluten-free grains and pseudo-cereals, such as:

- Amaranth
- Barley
- Buckwheat
- Corn (maize)
- Kamut
- Millet
- Oats
- Quinoa
- Rice
- Rye
- Sorghum
- Spelt
- Teff
- Triticale
- Wheat
- Wild rice

Grains Are Not Nutrient-Dense

One reason I personally avoid eating grains is there is far more nutrition in vegetables, fruits, good fats and high-quality meats than in grains.

Grains Are High in Carbs

Another reason I avoid grains is their high carbohydrate density. The carbohydrates in grains, and the processed foods that contain them, upset the blood glucose balance in the body. Grains are high in calories and sugars. Have you ever heard how cows are "fattened up" on grains? Well, that's because grain consumption in large quantities tends to lead to weight gain. Eating foods high in carbohydrates due to grain content causes insulin levels to spike, which can lead to diabetes.

Grains Irritate the Gut

Grains, especially those that contain gluten, are also gut irritants. Gut lining irritation keeps us from properly digesting our food and can lead to inflammation in our body. Inflammation is the root cause of many of our diseases of civilization. Thus, consuming large amounts of processed, grain-based foods puts you at a higher risk for autoimmune diseases, cancer and other health problems.

LEGUMES

For some reason, saying I do not consume legumes causes the strongest reaction; the idea of not eating legumes just perplexes people. While I can't give you a dissertation on all the reasons for not eating legumes, I can give a high-level explanation for why they are not included in the Paleo template.

First of all, while legumes contain protein, they are not a source of complete protein and are primarily a source of carbohydrates. These carbohydrates are not easily broken down in our body, which is why beans are famous for causing gas. There are ways to reduce this problem by properly preparing beans by soaking and/or fermenting them. But generally speaking, I prefer to consume more nutrient-dense foods, such as meat, fish, vegetables, fruits, nuts and seeds.

The legume family also includes peanuts and soybeans. We all know how allergenic peanuts are for many individuals. They are often grown with pesticides and come in highly processed forms, often with tremendous amounts of artificial additives. My older son is very allergic to both peanuts and soy. I also have, minimally, an oral allergy to legumes, so giving them up for our family was not difficult.

DAIRY

While I am far from being a vegetarian, when it comes to an interest in the humane treatment of animals, we do find common ground. Commercial, factory-farmed cattle, including dairy cattle, are often kept in inhumane conditions. In addition to being subjected to less-than-ideal living conditions, factory-farmed cattle are routinely given synthetic hormones. They are also fed an unnatural diet that includes soybeans and corn, as well as by-products from other animals—even candy, wrappers and all! Feeding animals that were created to eat grass something other than grass as the main part of their diet makes them sick. To try to prevent this from happening, factory-farmed cattle are often pumped full of antibiotics. They are also exposed to pesticides and other environmental toxins that then make their way into the dairy products.

CONSIDER TRYING A THIRTY-DAY ELIMINATION PERIOD TO HELP DETERMINE YOUR TOLERANCE OF DAIRY PRODUCTS. FOLLOW WITH REINTRODUCTION OF DAIRY PRODUCTS AND MONITOR YOUR REACTIONS.

Lactose and Casein in Dairy

In addition to the food-quality issues related to dairy, many people are sensitive to the sugar and proteins found therein. Lactose is the sugar component of milk and intolerance happens when it is not digested properly. The symptoms of lactose intolerance are bloating and gastrointestinal upset. Casein and whey are proteins found in milk products. Both of these proteins can cause problematic symptoms for people who often do not realize dairy is the trigger. Casein especially, which has some similarities to gluten, can cause reactions in gluten-sensitive individuals (especially those with celiac disease).

The Health Benefits of Grass-Fed Butter and Ghee

If you find you are able to tolerate dairy, either in the form of ghee or in real butter, you will be happy to know they are both highly nutritious foods. A tablespoon of ghee contains 8 grams of saturated fatty acid (SFA), 3.7 grams of monounsaturated fatty acid (MFA) and 0.5 grams of polyunsaturated fatty acid (PUFA). Saturated fat, contrary to what you might have learned, is not an evil menace directly responsible for heart disease. Monounsaturated fats (also known as oleic acid) are the main structural fats of the body and are nontoxic even at high doses. Butter and ghee from pasture-raised animals are also rich in fat-soluble vitamins, such as A, D and K2, as well as conjugated linoleic acid (CLA). CLA, an essential fatty acid found almost exclusively in grass-fed animals, may protect against cancer, heart disease and type 2 diabetes. Using organic butter may ensure you are avoiding hormones and pesticides that could end up in your ghee. (For more information on butter and ghee, see page 20.)

Grain-Free Cooking and Baking

Gluten-free cooking and baking is very popular these days. While not all gluten-free flours are grain free, all grain-free flours are automatically gluten free. It can be tricky to get the ratios of flours, starches, fats, proteins, sugars and liquids just right in recipes, and this is especially true in grain-free cooking and baking. But after several years of practice, I believe I have mastered the basics and even some highly advanced preparations. Many pounds of almond flour, butter, coconut oil and eggs have been sacrificed in the development of these recipes, which required many iterations and tweaking to get them just right. Grain-free flours do not produce results identical to standard, wheat-flour-based products. But in many cases these desserts and treats are superior, not only in nutrition but in taste, to more highly processed foods. I recommend you stick to my original recipe the first time you make them, before trying substitutions (other than the ones recommended in the recipes).

Ingredients, Tools & Tips

KEY INGREDIENTS

This is a list of key ingredients you will need when making the recipes in this book.

Coconut

IS COCONUT REALLY A NUT?

Many of the recipes in this book use coconut products. For this reason it is important to understand more about this versatile food and its many derivatives. Coconuts are not technically nuts. Sometimes they are referred to as pseudo-nuts, but they are actually large seeds from the palm family that are classified as drupes. While the American College of Allergy, Asthma and Immunology (ACAAI) does not recognize coconut as a nut, the US Food and Drug Administration (FDA) considers it to be a tree nut. However, while it is possible for some individuals to have an allergy to both tree nuts and coconut, it is not common. Please speak with your allergist before consuming coconut-based products if you have tree nut allergies or other serious food allergies.

HEALTH BENEFITS OF COCONUT

Over the years, coconut has gotten a bad rap. In fact, there was an effort years ago to replace coconut oil on the market with hydrogenated oils and trans fats. But these days, people are starting to recognize that coconut products are actually highly nutritious. Coconut oil, for example, is high in medium-chain triglycerides (MCTs), which are more rapidly absorbed by the body and more quickly metabolized (burned) as fuel. The result is that instead of being stored as fat, the calories contained in MCTs are very efficiently converted into fuel for immediate use by organs and muscles. The lauric acid in coconut has anti-inflammatory properties, which is especially important for individuals with autoimmune diseases. It also has been shown to boost immune function and heart health. Polyphenols, which are powerful antioxidants, are also found in high quantities in coconut. Coconut flour is high in fiber and low in carbohydrates, making it a good choice for individuals trying to maintain their blood sugar levels.

These are just a few of the health benefits of this amazing natural product. Let's take a look at the different forms coconut takes, many of which are ingredients found in numerous recipes in this book.

COCONUT PRODUCTS

Coconut products come in many forms and the terms and definitions can be confusing. But coconut is a highly nutritious and stable food with a delicious flavor, useful in all its forms as an ingredient in many recipes. The fat from coconut remains stable at high temperatures, meaning it is not easily broken down to become oxidized and harmful. It is great as a substitute for butter or ghee if you are unable to tolerate dairy products or if you stick to a strictly vegan diet.

Coconut Milk

Coconut milk is produced by combining the flesh of coconuts with water. Baking with coconut milk is wonderful because of the high fat content. I almost always use organic, full-fat coconut milk in baking. Occasionally, light coconut milk, which is lower in fat, is preferable for such things as smoothies and shakes, depending on the fat content of other ingredients. Coconut milk beverages sold in a carton are useful in a pinch but with so many additives, they are definitely not optimal.

Coconut Cream

Just like coconut milk, coconut cream comes from the pressing of fresh coconut meat, but is much thicker and richer with much less water. Coconut cream has a distinct coconut flavor and highly creamy texture, making it great for extra thickness in recipes. Its high fat content makes coconut cream ideal for whipping into a topping much like traditional dairy whipped cream. Leaving a can of full-fat coconut milk in the refrigerator overnight is a good way to separate the coconut cream from the coconut water. But you can increasingly find coconut cream sold separately either in grocery stores or online.

Creamed Coconut

Creamed coconut may sound like a synonym for *coconut cream* but, confusingly, it is a totally different product. Creamed coconut is coconut flesh that has been pulverized and formed into solid blocks. It is an extremely concentrated form of coconut and is often used to flavor curries. I have used creamed coconut to thicken coconut cream pies, but it is one form of coconut that I just happen to use least often in dessert recipes.

> **WATCH OUT:** Cream of coconut is not the same as coconut cream (or even creamed coconut, for that matter). The term typically describes a presweetened version of coconut cream used for desserts and mixed drinks. For this reason cream of coconut is not interchangeable with coconut cream.

Coconut Butter

Unlike coconut oil, which is the pure fat from the coconut, coconut butter is a spread made from the meat of the coconut. It is similar to other nut butters, such as almond or cashew butter. Even though it is not always as thick and the texture will vary from jar to jar, it can often be used in recipes as a substitute for nut butters. Coconut butter is a great option for people allergic to tree nuts (see "Is Coconut Really a Nut?" on page 11). Jars of coconut butter do not need refrigeration and may be stored at room temperature. It is often necessary to reheat the coconut butter prior to use and stir the coconut oil back into the coconut butter for a smooth, creamy consistency. Be careful when reheating coconut butter because it can burn easily.

Coconut Flakes, Shredded Coconut and Desiccated Coconut

All three of these products are very similar. Coconut flakes are dried coconut that comes in flat, wide pieces. Shredded coconut is similar but is, as the name implies, shredded. It comes in thin strands or strips. Both coconut flakes and shredded coconut retain some moisture. Desiccated coconut on the other hand, is very finely ground coconut with most of the moisture removed. This is not to be confused with coconut flour, which has the fat removed. I recommend organic, unsweetened coconut flakes and shreds.

More Coconut Products

For information on coconut flour, coconut oil and coconut sugars, see the appropriate sections in "Key Ingredients."

Flours, Starches and Nut Meals

Of the many different types of gluten-free flours on the market, only a few are also grain free. The following ingredients are the ones I rely on most for grain-free baking and in other recipes. You will find these ingredients used time and again alone or in combination, depending on the nature of the recipe.

ALMOND FLOUR (BLANCHED)

Almond flour is produced by finely grinding raw, blanched almonds. The flour is very fine and produces baked goods with a very smooth texture. For best results, use blanched almond flour for most of the recipes in this book that call for almond flour. High-quality blanched almond flour is becoming more commonly available in local stores. However, ordering it online is a great way to save money on this nutritious, versatile flour. You can also try making it yourself (see "How to Make Almond Flour/Meal," page 32).

ALMOND MEAL

Compared to blanched almond flour, almond meal has a coarser texture due to the fact that the skin of the

almond is ground along with the nut. Almond meal is best used in more rustic recipes, such as Paleo Breakfast Porridge (page 61) or Almond Crumble (page 107). For baked goods, almond meal produces a heavier, oilier end product.

COCONUT FLOUR

Ground from dried, defatted coconut meat, coconut flour is an ideal gluten-free, grain-free flour. It is also high in fiber and low in digestible carbohydrates. Two tablespoons of coconut flour delivers 5 grams of fiber with only 8 grams of carbs. This makes it an excellent choice for keeping blood sugar from going off the charts when using it in a dessert or sweet treat recipe. For persons with allergies or intolerances to nuts, coconut flour is a terrific alternative. And because nut flours are high in omega-6 fats, opting for coconut flour in recipes by itself or in combination with other grain-free flours, where it works well, helps with the ratio of fats. Coconut flour is not considered to be a raw product. You should store coconut flour in an airtight container in the refrigerator to keep it fresh.

Cooking with Coconut Flour

Coconut flour is extremely dry and does not work in recipes in the same way as standard wheat flour so you must be careful when trying to make substitutions. A good rule of thumb is to use one-quarter the amount of coconut flour of what would normally be used with wheat flour. Because a little goes a long way, it is important to measure your coconut flour. One teaspoon too much can result in products that are too dense and dry, whereas using too little coconut flour will keep your product from holding together. You will notice recipes that use primarily coconut flour also rely on a rather large number of eggs to balance the dryness of the flour.

ARROWROOT AND TAPIOCA

Arrowroot and tapioca are gluten free and grain free flours, ground from starchy tubers. Both the terms *flour* and *starch* are used to describe the same product. Arrowroot and tapioca flours are higher in carbohydrates than either nut flours or coconut flour. Even though arrowroot and tapioca are different, I find them to be virtually interchangeable in many recipes. I often use smaller amounts in concert with almond or coconut flours or when I am determined to create a nut-free recipe that is otherwise difficult to achieve with just coconut flour.

Arrowroot Flour

Arrowroot flour is neutral tasting and tolerates acidic ingredients, such as citrus. You can bake with arrowroot but it is best in recipes that use lower temperatures because it starts to break down at higher temperatures, such as in a boiling sauce. Arrowroot flour dissolves easily in liquid and freezes well but is not ideal in dairy-based sauces.

Tapioca Flour

Like arrowroot, tapioca flour is slightly sweet to the taste and helps bind gluten- and grain-free recipes together. It works wonders for the texture of baked goods. It makes the Dessert Pizza Crust (page 127) crispy and adds a little more spring and elasticity to the Almond Raspberry Muffins (page 42). Tapioca does not break down at high temperatures, works well as a thickener for sauces and pie fillings and can be refrigerated or frozen with no problem.

FLAXSEED MEAL

Flax is often touted for its healthful components such as omega-3 essential fatty acids, lignans and fiber. I like to use flaxseed meal in such recipes as Paleo Breakfast Porridge (page 61) and to make flax eggs (see "Egg Alternatives," page 26), when I am looking for an egg-free alternative in baking. It is best to keep whole flaxseeds in the refrigerator and then grind them right before use, to ensure freshness.

Sweeteners
UNREFINED SUGAR

In contrast to refined sugar, unrefined sugar is sugar that has not undergone extensive processing. The word *unrefined* is a bit of a misnomer in that most have been processed in some way or other. However, unrefined sugar retains many of the nutrients that it had before its minimal processing, which means there is a reason to put it in your body other than just its taste. Without the chemical processing, there is also less chance you will be consuming something that is hazardous to your health.

Examples of unrefined sugar ingredients in *Sweet Paleo*:

Raw Honey

Raw honey is the most Paleo, and arguably the most healthful, of all the sweeteners used in recipes in this book. It has long been an important part of the human diet and was the only concentrated sweetener available for much of human history. Increasing evidence indicates honey has uniquely beneficial physiological effects. Honey contains enzymes, other proteins, trace minerals, flavonoids and other healthful components. Supplementing with a few tablespoons of honey per day increases antioxidant levels and reduces inflammation. Honey also has antibacterial, antiviral and antitumor effects, among other benefits. Consuming a bit of honey every day can be part of a healthful diet, especially when you eat raw honey, which has more enzymes and nutrients.

Alternatives to Honey

Coconut sugar, maple sugar and molasses are popular alternative natural sweeteners. They all contain minerals, such as calcium, zinc and iron and are lower on the glycemic index than white sugar. Coconut sugar is the lowest, at 35. All three are better alternatives to refined sugar and are natural and minimally processed and contain minerals and phytonutrients. They also have favorable fructose-to-glucose ratios, which can be important for those with gut issues or fructose intolerance.

COCONUT NECTAR/SAP

Nutrient-rich coconut nectar (or sap) is abundant in seventeen amino acids, broad-spectrum B vitamins, vitamin C and such minerals as magnesium and potassium. Coconut nectar also contains prebiotic fiber, which promotes digestive health. It is also much lower in fructose (about 1.5 percent compared to 40 to 90 percent in agave nectar) and less processed than agave. Coconut sugar is also considered a sustainable food. Once you tap the tree, the sap flows from it for another twenty years. A tree cannot produce both coconuts and sap. So, there is some economic controversy regarding its use.

COCONUT SUGAR (A.K.A. COCONUT CRYSTALS)

Coconut sugar, also known as coconut palm sugar or coconut crystals, is made from the sap of the coconut palm that has been extracted, boiled and dehydrated. It is different from palm sugar, which comes from the sugar palm tree. Coconut sugar is caramel color and has a taste similar to that of brown sugar. It can be substituted for regular cane sugar in most recipes but will lend a darker color and richer taste. Coconut sugar is high in sucrose, with low levels of fructose and glucose.

MAPLE SYRUP

Made from sap collected from mature maple trees, maple syrup is a pure, natural and sustainable sweetener. It is categorized and graded according to color, clarity, density and strength of maple flavor. Grade A is most common and comes in light, medium and dark varieties with varying degrees of color and intensity. Grade B maple syrup is amber in color and much darker than Grade A. It has a stronger, more pronounced maple flavor.

> **WATCH OUT:** The pure maple syrup recommended for recipes in this book should not be confused with pancake syrup. Imitation maple syrup is an artificial food made from potentially harmful ingredients, such as high-fructose corn syrup and caramel coloring.

HONEY VS. MAPLE SYRUP

Many of the recipes in this book give the option of using either honey or maple syrup as an ingredient. The primary reason for this is because not everyone chooses to eat both honey and maple syrup— instead preferring the flavor of one over the other or having one on hand versus another. Vegans especially will likely not choose to use honey, due to its being produced by bees, but will opt for maple syrup or other vegan sweeteners. It is important to keep in mind that although honey and maple syrup can be used interchangeably in some recipes, they are not identical either in their level of sweetness, moisture content or nutrition. Honey and pure maple syrup each have advantages and disadvantages. Maple syrup is higher in minerals and lower in fructose. Honey, on the other hand, is a good choice for more vitamins, especially raw honey in uncooked preparations.

Here is a chart to help differentiate the two commonly used sweeteners.

SWEETENER	CALORIES	SUGAR	NUTRITION
1 tablespoon honey	64	17.4 g of carbs (17.3 g from sugars); primarily fructose with smaller amounts of glucose and sucrose	Higher than maple syrup in vitamins B6 and C and riboflavin. Raw honey contains beneficial enzymes.
1 tablespoon pure maple syrup	52	13.5 g of carbs (12.4 g from sugars); primarily sucrose	Higher than honey in minerals, including iron, calcium, zinc, manganese, potassium and sodium.

MAPLE SUGAR

Just as the name suggests, maple sugar, like maple syrup, comes from the sap of the maple tree. To produce maple sugar, the sap is boiled until the water has been removed and the sugar has crystallized. Granulated maple sugar can be used like standard sugar except it is sweeter and more concentrated. Often one must reduce the amount of maple sugar in recipes to avoid an overly sweet end product. Just like maple syrup, maple sugar has a strong maple flavor and aroma. It is a fairly expensive product, so I save it for recipes where it makes a real flavor impact or there is a need for a dry, granulated sugar instead of a liquid alternative. Maple sugar is usually lighter in color and sometimes drier than coconut sugar, so I prefer to use it in recipes where I don't want to darken the color of the final product. If the granules of the maple sugar are too large for an application, you can use a coffee grinder to create a finer sugar.

MOLASSES

Molasses is a dense, viscous by-product of the processing of sugar cane and sugar beet into table sugar. Molasses contains high levels of potassium, calcium, vitamin B6, iron and magnesium in just a tablespoon. It is excellent in giving a rich, complex flavor to such things as gingerbread cookies or pecan pie filling.

DATES

Medjool dates are moist, plump and luscious little nuggets of nutrition, flavor and texture. They contain more potassium than bananas and are high in soluble and insoluble fiber. Dates are also high in B vitamins, magnesium and iron. I find them especially useful in making such things as unbaked tart crusts and for adding moisture and texture to cakes and ice creams. As a type of fruit, it comes as no surprise that dates are relatively high in fructose.

REFINED SUGARS

Sugar that has been highly refined offers only empty calories lacking in nutrients and minerals. Some have gone through a chemical refining process. I use a couple of different varieties primarily for decorative purposes.

Turbinado Sugar

Turbinado sugar is made from the initial pressing of sugar cane. More of the natural molasses remains in the crystals because it is less processed. Turbinado sugar does rank a bit lower in calories than white cane sugar, mainly because it carries more moisture, not because there is something inherently healthier about it. I typically only use turbinado sugar as a finishing sugar, such as to top scones (okay, not truly needed) for extra crunch.

Powdered or Confectioners' Sugar

Powdered sugar and confectioners' sugar are the same thing: a very finely ground version of white sugar that sometimes contains an anticaking agent. This type of sugar is often used to make icings and frostings. It can be a bit shocking to find how many cups of powdered sugar are called for in many standard dessert recipes and frostings, especially when compared with the much lower amount of sugar used in *Sweet Paleo* recipes. In fact, you will find confectioners' sugar used in just a few recipes and only as a slight dusting, for primarily decorative purposes.

Other Popular Sweeteners Not Used in *Sweet Paleo*

The sweeteners listed here are the ones I tend to rely on for my recipes. However, a few other sweeteners on the market could be considered appropriate for Paleo recipes. For example, stevia is a popular natural sweetener but something I rarely use. I have no real opposition to stevia; I simply do not particularly enjoy the taste and am not experienced in using it in recipes. I stay away from agave nectar as it is highly processed, has little nutritional value and has a very high fructose content. Agave may be used as a substitute for raw honey by individuals who do not like the taste of honey or who are vegans and thus oppose the use of honey.

Fats and Oils

Fats and oils are the most calorie-dense sources of nutrition in our diets. So it makes sense to be mindful of the quality of the fats we are taking into our body, especially with recipes like the ones in this book that rely heavily on fat ingredients. You will not find highly processed vegetable oils or trans fats recommended here. Even if you are making a dessert that will be eaten in moderation, you can ensure it contains fat and oil ingredients that are more natural and healthful. There are other saturated and unsaturated fats and oils that I would consider healthful, but the following are the ones you will find most often in the recipes in this book.

AVOCADO

It may seem strange to include an ingredient that is often associated with savory dishes, such as guacamole, in a sweets and desserts cookbook. But ripe avocado is an amazingly versatile food that lends itself to use in frostings, pies, cakes and mousses. When paired with strong flavors, such as cocoa or lime, the mild flavor of avocado is virtually undetectable and you are left with an end product high in healthful, dairy-free fat.

COCONUT OIL
Refined Coconut Oil

Most of the coconut oils commonly available in grocery stores are refined. This type of coconut oil is rather tasteless and odorless, which makes it useful in cooking foods where you do not want a strong coconut flavor. Refined coconut oils do not offer the same health benefits of a virgin, completely raw coconut oil, but they are still sources of beneficial fatty acids.

> **WATCH OUT:** If you choose to use refined coconut oil, make sure it does not contain ingredients that have gone through a chemical distillation process using harsh solvents, or are made from rancid oil by-products or have been hydrogenated or partially hydrogenated.

Unrefined, Virgin Coconut Oil

When using coconut oil in a recipe, I choose to use the unrefined, virgin, cold-pressed variety. It is more expensive than refined coconut oil and has a stronger coconut flavor. But the mildest-tasting virgin oils have been extracted from coconut at low temperatures. You can save money by buying virgin coconut oil in bulk because it remains fresh for long periods of time—six months or more.

Storage for Coconut Oil: You should keep coconut oil stored in a cool, dark place. If you refrigerate coconut oil, it will become extremely hard and difficult to scoop. In the cooler months of the year, it is more solid even at room temperature. I can always tell when the warmer months are upon us when my coconut oil is completely liquid in its container.

How to Liquefy Coconut Oil: If your coconut oil is solid at room temperature or has been refrigerated, you will need to melt or "liquefy" the oil before using it in most recipes. I typically do this in the microwave until just melted but you can also do this by immersing a small jar of coconut oil in warm water for several minutes until liquefied. For most recipes you want coconut oil that is liquid but not too hot or it may cook some of the ingredients while mixing together.

PALM SHORTENING

Palm shortening is derived from palm oil. Unlike vegetable oil shortening (Crisco, for example) palm shortening is not hydrogenated and contains no trans-fatty acids. It has a firm texture and a high melting point, is very shelf stable and is colorless and odorless so it will not affect the taste of a recipe. If a recipe calls for butter, you can most likely substitute organic palm shortening as a dairy-free alternative. Coconut oil is not a good substitute for palm shortening in frostings and other products that need to be more solid at room temperature.

BUTTER

Butter has been a part of the human diet for thousands of years. It is one of the oldest and most natural foods on the planet. Butter is a dairy product made by churning fresh or fermented milk or cream—cow's milk is the most common. Butter contains about 80 percent fat; the rest is water and milk solids, such as lactose and casein. When these recipes call for butter, be sure it is unsalted, preferably pastured butter.

GHEE

Also known as clarified butter, butter oil or drawn butter, ghee is a delicious, healthful fat, especially when it is made from pasture butter from grass-fed cows. Even if you find you need to avoid dairy, most likely you can still enjoy ghee. Ghee is butter that has had the water and milk solids, such as lactose, casein and whey, removed. It is somewhat different from clarified butter in that the process of making ghee involves toasting the milk solids, resulting in a nutty, rich flavor. Unlike butter, ghee has a long shelf life and can be used for high-temperature cooking. It is also not as difficult to make as you might think (see "Homemade Ghee" on page 38).

WATCH OUT: Because ghee has had the water and milk solids removed, it does not work in recipes in exactly the same way as butter. However, generally speaking, the two are interchangeable in many recipes.

LARD

Lard is pork fat that has been rendered to be suitable for cooking. Contrary to modern conventional wisdom, lard is not only a glorious cooking and baking fat, it is actually very healthful. The best, most healthful lard comes from ethically raised, organic, free-range pigs. Be careful when buying commercially packaged lard as it often contains hydrogenated fats. Lard is high in vitamin D, which is a powerful immunity booster and aids in the absorption of calcium. It also has more than twice the monounsaturated fat as butter. It is also low in the omega-6 fatty acids, known to promote inflammation, yet has higher levels of omega-3 fatty acids. Not only is lard nutritious, it is terrific for baking. Leaf lard is the highest grade of lard and is prized by bakers for use in producing moist, flaky piecrusts. It comes from the visceral—or "soft"—fat from around the kidneys and loin of the pig. It lacks any real pork or meaty flavor, making it an excellent neutral-flavored cooking fat. You can substitute odorless, high-quality lard in many recipes as a replacement for butter and other fats.

Milk and Cheese

COW'S MILK

Even though most recipes in this book call for full-fat coconut milk, you can often substitute cow's milk if you consume dairy products. Just like all other dairy ingredients, I suggest you select organic, full-fat milk from cows that have been pasture raised (grass fed). I personally enjoy using raw and unpasteurized milk and milk products when possible.

GOAT CHEESE

Goat's milk contains lactose in almost the same amount as cow's milk. However, the fermentation process to make cheese reduces the amount of lactose, making it easier for people who are lactose-intolerant to eat. Goat cheese is better tolerated by some individuals who are otherwise unable to eat dairy products. Lactose intolerance is different from milk allergy where people are allergic to the protein in milk. This is more common with cow's milk and may explain why goat's milk is more easily tolerated by some. For this reason you will see a few recipes in this book that make use of goat cheese, also known as chèvre.

Sea Salt

Whenever salt is listed in this book, it refers to sea salt. Finely ground Celtic sea salt is my favorite. It is slightly moist and light gray in color. The salt is harvested off the coast of Brittany, France, using the Celtic method of wooden rakes and is naturally air- and sun-dried in clay ponds. Celtic sea salt is minimally processed and retains eighty-four trace minerals found in seawater, such as iodine, iron, calcium, magnesium, manganese, potassium and zinc. And unlike regular table salt, Celtic sea salt contains no preservatives or other additives.

Gelatin

Gelatin is the purified protein obtained from selected pieces of calf and cattle hides, demineralized cattle bones (ossein) and pork skin. That may sound disconcerting to some people, but this tasteless, odorless powder is a great dietary supplement supporting skin, hair and nail growth. It is also considered to be anti-inflammatory and may improve joint health. There are numerous culinary uses for gelatin, such as making homemade fruit snacks, stabilizing frostings (see Stabilized Whipped Coconut Cream, page 206) and

creating your own marshmallows! In certain recipes, such as Maple Marshmallows (page 183), gelatin is essential; in others, such as the dairy-free Basic Vanilla Bean Ice Cream (page 151), gelatin is optional. Typically, I use unflavored gelatin made from grass-fed beef cattle, which I purchase online. One tablespoon equals one envelope of gelatin.

Vanilla

Vanilla extract is a solution containing the flavor compound vanillin as the primary ingredient. High-quality, pure vanilla extract is extremely useful in baking and dessert recipes of all kinds. I find it especially useful in grain-free baking to help mellow out the coconut flavor of dishes that are high in coconut ingredients. The liquid version is the most common. Double vanilla is even more concentrated and vanilla powder is useful in recipes where added liquid might be detrimental.

Chocolate
COCOA POWDER

Cocoa beans are roasted, then ground to a paste. The thick paste is pressed between hydraulic plates that squeeze out about half of the excess cocoa butter. What's left is a hard disk of cocoa powder, which is then grated into a fine powder. Most cocoa powders are between 20 and 22 percent fat. Cocoa powder is highly nutritious and can provide numerous health benefits. Cocoa's bad reputation is the result of such additives as high amounts of refined sugar and other problematic ingredients, and not of the cocoa itself.

PREPARED CHOCOLATE

An exception to the "no refined sugar" designation of the recipes in *Sweet Paleo* is chocolate. While many recipes use cocoa powder and something like honey or maple syrup for sweetness, there are times when simply melting a few allergy-friendly, dark chocolate chips makes the most sense. And of course, it would be difficult to make chocolate chip cookies without the chips (or chocolate chunks)! However, when cooking with prepared chocolate I almost always use dark chocolate (higher than 70% cacao) because it has less sugar. You can also find allergy-friendly chocolate chips that are soy- and dairy-free (Enjoy Life brand is one example).

Eggs

I would love nothing better than to raise my own chickens. I have visions of different breeds of chickens living peacefully together, roaming freely on pasture, eating their natural diet and faithfully laying eggs for our family. But until that day arrives, I will have to be satisfied with buying the best eggs I can find in neighboring farms.

EGG QUALITY

Many of the recipes in this book contain eggs and in some cases *lots* of eggs. When consuming eggs, it is important to understand the difference among the types available for purchase. Health-conscious consumers know to look for such designations as "organic," "free-range," "pastured" and "cage free," but while it may seem as though these terms are interchangeable, they are not. The best eggs are the free-range eggs often referred to as "pasture-raised." These eggs come from hens that roam freely outdoors on pasture, where they can forage for a natural diet that includes seeds, green plants, insects, worms and the occasional small rodent. The flavor of these eggs is unmatched with their bright yellow (almost orange!) yolks that are higher in vitamins A and E, omega-3s and other nutrients.

EGG TEMPERATURE

For most recipes using eggs, it is best to allow them to come to room temperature before using. Meringues will whip easier and with much larger volume when using room-temperature eggs. Cold eggs tend to chill such ingredients as liquefied coconut oil or melted butter or ghee, making it difficult to evenly mix them into a batter. Letting eggs sit out on the counter for thirty minutes should do the trick. You can also allow them to sit in tepid water to speed up the process.

EGG SIZES

Egg sizes can vary drastically. When buying eggs in a grocery store, you will find they are typically sorted and labeled by size. However, that is not always the case with pasture-raised eggs you buy from a local farm or that come from your own backyard chickens. The following tables will provide a guide for what is meant

by the size designations. You can assume the recipes in this book use large eggs. But keep in mind what is considered "large" in the USA is not the same in Europe or in other parts of the world. When in doubt, you may choose to weigh your eggs for a given recipe to achieve the best results. (The volumes given are for an egg itself without the shell.)

MODERN EGG SIZES (USA)	MASS PER EGG	COOKING YIELD (VOLUME)
Jumbo	>2.5 oz or 71 g	59 ml or 4 tablespoons
Very large to extra large	2.25 oz or 64 g	56 ml or 3.7 tablespoons
Large	2 oz or 57 g	46 ml or 3.25 tablespoons
Medium	1.75 oz or 50 g	43 ml or 3 tablespoons
Small	1.5 oz or 43 g	39 ml or 2.6 tablespoons
Peewee	1.25 oz or 35 g	33 ml or 2.2 tablespoons

EGG SIZES IN EUROPE	MASS PER EGG
Very large	73 g and over
Large	63 to 73 g
Medium	53 to 63 g
Small	53 g or under

Egg White Sizes

1 large egg white = 2 tablespoons = 1 ounce = 30 grams

EGG SUBSTITUTIONS

It is possible to make substitutions for eggs in some recipes. Coconut flour recipes are especially reliant on eggs to counteract the dryness of the flour. If a recipe contains numerous eggs paired with coconut flour, I do not recommend trying to re-create the recipe with egg substitutes or equivalents. The same would be true for pastries, such as pâte à choux. However, in some recipes that use one or two eggs, it might be possible to use a substitute successfully.

EGG EQUIVALENTS	EQUIVALENT
1 whole large egg	2 large egg yolks plus 1 tablespoon cold water
	3½ tablespoons thawed frozen egg
	2½ tablespoons powdered egg white plus 2 tablespoons water
1 large egg white	2 tablespoons thawed frozen egg white
	1 tablespoon powdered egg white plus 2 tablespoons water

Egg Alternatives

FLAX EGGS

Makes Equivalent of 1 large egg

1 tablespoon flaxseeds   3 tablespoons water

Grind the flaxseeds into meal with a food processor, spice grinder or mortar and pestle. Add the water, stir and allow the mixture to rest until it becomes gelatinous.

CHIA SEED EGG SUBSTITUTE

Makes Equivalent of 1 large egg

1 tablespoon chia seeds   3 tablespoons water

Grind the chia seeds into meal with a food processor, spice grinder or mortar and pestle. Add the water, stir and allow the mixture to rest until it becomes gelatinous.

WATCH OUT: I have not tried the recipes using egg substitutes and cannot guarantee the results.

Ingredient Substitutions

CORNSTARCH SUBSTITUTE

You can substitute 2 tablespoons of tapioca flour for each 1 tablespoon of cornstarch in conventional recipes.

CREAM OF TARTAR SUBSTITUTE

Use an equal amount of white vinegar or fresh lemon juice.

LEAVENING SUBSTITUTE

One teaspoon of baking powder equals ⅓ teaspoon of baking soda or ⅔ teaspoon of cream of tartar.

VEGAN ALTERNATIVES

Alternatives to Honey

Vegans eschew animal products of any kind. For this reason, even raw honey is off limits. Even though I do not generally recommend agave nectar, it is one option for vegans to use as a sweetener in recipes that call for honey. All of the other sweeteners listed in this book are vegan-friendly.

Alternatives to Gelatin

Vegans and vegetarians alike will choose not to eat gelatin, which is an animal product. Gelatin is used in several recipes as a thickener. However, in most cases vegans and vegetarians may either substitute agar (a.k.a. agar-agar) for the gelatin or leave it out entirely.

THE IMPORTANCE OF WEIGHING INGREDIENTS

In developing and testing recipes for this book, I made sure to adhere to a system of weights for each of the various flours and starches. Weighing dry ingredients for grain-free baking is essential for consistent results. Just a little too much or a bit too little of a particular ingredient can drastically change the results. I use grams when weighing flours, starches and cocoa powder because it gives me the most accurate measurement. I recommend using a digital kitchen scale for the task and to get into the habit of weighing your ingredients. (See the "Flour Weight" for a list of weights used in this cookbook and the equivalent cup volume.)

Even though I have cross-referenced these weights across many different sources, there may not be consistent agreement from everyone on what constitutes a cup of blanched almond flour, for example. However, if you are using a recipe in this book, weighing out the flours in these amounts given will produce the best results.

FLOUR WEIGHT	1 TBSP	¼ CUP	⅓ CUP	½ CUP	⅔ CUP	¾ CUP	1 CUP
Coconut flour	7 g	28 g	37 g	64 g	75 g	84 g	112 g
Almond flour	6.25 g	25 g	33 g	50 g	67 g	75 g	100 g
Tapioca or arrowroot flour	8 g	32 g	43 g	64 g	85 g	96 g	128 g
Cocoa powder	8 g	32 g	43 g	64 g	85 g	96 g	128 g

KITCHEN EQUIPMENT

BAKING SHEETS

Sheet pans are great for baking cookies, toasting nuts and spreading out such things as melted chocolate for chocolate bark. I find that for most recipes I use a half sheet pan with standard dimensions 13 x 18 inches.

CANDY THERMOMETER

The mere mention of the need for a thermometer is often enough to dissuade someone from bothering to try a recipe. But thermometers, like kitchen scales, are your friend. It takes the guesswork out of when a sugar solution has reached the required stage of cooking.

FOOD PROCESSOR

One of the first investments I made in kitchen appliances after going Paleo was a large food processor. I use my 11-cup Cuisinart to grind nuts, mix tart crusts and cookie doughs as well as to grate carrots and zucchini for veggie-filled cakes and breads. I would definitely rank a quality food processor as one of the most important tools in a Paleo kitchen.

ICE CREAM MAKER

If you love homemade ice creams, custards and sorbets, then you should consider investing in an ice cream machine. Making your own frozen treats is especially necessary for those of us with intolerance to dairy products.

KITCHEN SCALE

Having a good kitchen scale, preferably a digital one, is practically indispensable for perfect results every time. This is especially true with gluten-free, grain-free baking. All the recipes in this book provide measurements in cups and grams for flours, starches and cocoa powder. You should get into the habit of weighing your flours before adding them to a recipe for more consistent results.

LOAF PAN

Gluten-free and grain-free baked goods rise differently than conventional baked goods. Investing in a narrower pan will do wonders for your final result. I have found that a 7½ x 3½-inch pan works especially well, allowing quick breads to cook more evenly and rise properly for better browning.

PASTRY BAGS AND TIPS

Pastry bags and tips come in handy for decorating cakes and cupcakes but also for piping dough onto a baking pan for such things as pâte à choux pastry and ladyfingers. You can use either disposable pastry bags or the reusable, plastic-coated bags. Large round and star tips are the most useful. If you do not have a pastry bag, for most recipes you can use a large resealable plastic bag with a bottom corner cut off.

PARCHMENT PAPER

Parchment paper is oil- and moisture-resistant paper made especially for oven use. It can be used to line cake molds and baking sheets and pans to keep food from sticking. Because I do not use the standard process of greasing, then using a layer of wheat flour to coat baking pans, parchment paper is a great option for nonstick baking—especially with gluten-free, grain-free recipes. Keep in mind parchment paper is not the same thing as waxed paper which is not meant to be heated and may melt or even ignite if used in the oven.

ROLLING PIN

You will need a good rolling pin when making such recipes as dessert pizza crust, cinnamon rolls, and cookies, such as Linzer cookies and chocolate shortbread. A rolling pin helps to efficiently roll out the dough and create a smooth, even surface.

SILICONE MATS AND MOLDS

Instead of parchment paper, another option is to use silicone mats on your baking sheets (Silpat is a well-known brand). Silicone mats are washable and reusable and do not leach any harmful chemicals when heated. They are great for baking but not for use when broiling food. Silicone molds for cupcakes and muffins are especially useful with grain-free baked goods, which have a tendency to stick to regular paper liners.

STAND MIXER

I have a place under the kitchen counter for it, but my stand mixer is rarely there—mainly because it is a constant fixture on top of my counter. The mixer gets a lot of use, whipping egg whites into meringue, turning coconut cream into a dreamy whipped topping and basic mixing of quick breads, cakes, macaroons, pâte à choux pastry dough and more. For most recipes, however, a hand mixer will also do the trick.

TART PANS AND PIE DISHES

A standard pie pan is 9 inches in diameter and 1¼ inches deep with sloping sides. Deep-dish pie pans are 1½ to 2 inches deep. Unlike pie pans, tart pans come in all sorts of shapes and sizes. They can be round or rectangular, and range anywhere from 4 to 12 inches across and from ¾ to 2 inches deep (smaller than 4 inches would be a tartlet pan). The best tart pans have a removable bottom that allows easier removal of the tart, resulting in a more formal presentation. My round classic fluted tart pan is 9½ inches in diameter and 1 inch high. The rectangular pan is 13¾ x 4½ inches and 1 inch high. Each of the tart pans I use holds approximately 4 cups, including the crust. This is the same volume as a standard 9 x 1¼-inch pie pan.

TUTORIALS AND GUIDES

Some recipes and processes are used over and over again in the course of making gluten-free and grain-free desserts, treats and other dishes. The following tutorials will provide guidance in some of those key processes and recipes for making the ingredients you will find used frequently in this cookbook.

HOW TO MAKE A MERINGUE

There are a few important things to know when making meringue (whipped egg whites).

- Be sure your bowl and whisk are very clean, with no oily residue. There must be absolutely no yolk in the whites. To ensure this, separate each egg white into a small bowl, then add it to the rest of the whites. That way, if a bit of yolk gets in with the white, you can save the egg for another purpose without ruining the entire batch of whites.

- A small amount of cream of tartar (or its equivalent; see page 27) helps egg whites whip. Using too much will have the opposite effect, however. A good rule of thumb is to use ⅛ teaspoon of cream of tartar for each large egg white. Add the cream of tartar as soon as the beaten egg white begins to foam—after about 1 minute of beating. Start on low speed and gradually increase the speed to medium-high.

- Unpasteurized egg whites are the easiest to use in making meringue. However, when using eggs that have not been pasteurized, it will be necessary to heat them enough to kill any harmful bacteria that might make someone ill. This can be done in a few different ways. In some recipes it is recommended that you whisk the eggs for a few minutes in a bowl set on a pot of simmering water (double-boiler method). This produces what is generally known as Swiss meringue. In other recipes, such as to make Italian Meringue Buttercream (page 209), you will essentially pasteurize the egg whites with hot sugar syrup. Otherwise, baking meringue, such as atop a pie or tart, for longer than 10 minutes in a 350°F oven should do the trick. When in doubt, you can try using pasteurized egg whites instead.

- If you use pasteurized egg whites to create meringues, they will not beat to sufficient stiffness unless either cream of tartar or an equivalent is added. You will need double the cream of tartar (to about ¼ teaspoon per large egg white) if you use pasteurized eggs. Start beating on low speed and gradually increase the speed to high. Pasteurized eggs take longer to stiffen than do egg whites that have not been pasteurized and the end product will not produce quite the same volume.

- It is best to use room-temperature egg whites when making meringue because they will whip much easier and with greater volume. Leaving eggs out of the refrigerator for about 30 minutes should be sufficient.
- When beating egg whites, they are classified in three stages, according to the peaks they form when the beater is lifted: soft, firm and stiff peaks. Once you achieve stiff peaks, do not beat any further or else the meringue will begin to deflate.

HOW TO MAKE ALMOND FLOUR/MEAL

First, let me warn you, in case you don't already know, almond flour is expensive! While it is possible to make your own almond flour at home, I will caution that the results you will be able to achieve will not produce the exact same result as the fine, blanched almond flours on the market. But you can get fairly close and save some money by making almond flour yourself.

You can make your own almond flour a couple of different ways. The first, more complicated method, starts with whole, raw almonds.

- You will need to first blanch the almonds by placing them in a bowl and covering them with boiling water. Let the almonds sit in the water for about one minute. (Do not leave the almonds in the water for too long or they will become too soft to grind.)
- Next, strain and rinse the almonds. At this point the almonds should easily slip out of their skins.
- Allow the skinless, blanched almonds to dry completely, then place them in a food processor or high-speed blender and process them until they form a fine flour. You can sift out any large almond pieces and grind them again for even more flour.

An easier method is to buy raw, slivered almonds, which are sold already blanched, and use them to make the flour, thus avoiding the blanching step. In either case, using a food processor to grind the almonds will produce a grainier, heavier product, more similar to almond meal. That texture is fine for some products, such as chocolate chip cookies or porridge. But using a high-speed blender will produce finer results more akin to the commercially available fine blanched almond flours.

If money is no object and you desire perfect results without the hassle of making your own flour, I recommend Honeyville Blanched Almond Flour or Wellbee Foods Super Fine Almond Flour. These are the brands I used when testing the recipes in this book.

> **WATCH OUT:** Be careful when grinding your almonds that you do not overprocess and turn them into almond butter.

HOW TO MAKE NUT MILK

Nut milk is a great resource for those of us with sensitivities to dairy products. Unfortunately, the nut milks you can buy in the grocery store are often filled with ingredients you might not otherwise choose to have in your diet—such as gums, preservatives and added sugar. Making your own nut milks is not as difficult as you might think! Nut milk can be made from just about any type of nut. The most common nut milk is made from almonds but you can also use Brazil nuts, cashews, hazelnuts, macadamia nuts and more. Soaking nuts prior to making nut milk is important for a couple of reasons. Soaking makes nuts easier to digest and it also improves their flavor. Refer to "Soaking Times for Nut Milk" for the recommended soaking time for each kind of nut.

SOAKING TIMES FOR NUT MILK	SOAKING TIME
Almond	8 to 12 hours
Brazil nut	None needed
Cashew	2 hours
Hazelnut	8 hours
Macadamia	8 hours
Pecan	4 to 6 hours
Pistachio	None needed
Walnut	4 hours

The ratio of water to nuts is about two to one for a final product that is roughly the consistency of 2% milk. Homemade nut milk only lasts a few days in the refrigerator, so only make as much as you will drink in that time. On page 36 is a recommended recipe.

Using the Leftover Nut Meal

The meal left behind after straining out the milk can be spread out on a baking pan and baked at as low a temperature as you can set your oven, for two to three hours until completely dried. You can either freeze the dry meal or use it immediately in certain recipes that do not call for the finer, blanched almond flour often required in baked goods. The grainier nut meal texture would work well in the Paleo Breakfast Porridge (page 61).

Oven-Baked Bacon

Why is bacon even discussed in *Sweet Paleo*? You can use your crispy bacon as a part of Chocolate Ganache and Bacon Frosting (page 207) or Chocolate Bacon Almond Bark (page 177).

Prior to going Paleo, I did not cook bacon very often. Bacon was then a forbidden food because I ate "healthy." Well, times have changed, haven't they? I firmly believe it is possible for bacon to be part of a healthful diet, but with some caveats. Bacon is a part of my diet but it is not an everyday food. If you are eating bacon on a regular basis, try to buy from a source that is organic, humanely raised, and free of GMO feed, antibiotics and hormones. When I buy conventionally produced bacon, I buy only the nitrate-/nitrite-free variety.

Baking bacon in the oven is great for an easy cleanup, crispy bacon and there's no splattering on the stovetop to worry about.

1. Buy high-quality bacon—ideally organic, uncured (nitrite/nitrate-free) bacon from humanely raised pigs.
2. Lay out the bacon on either a sheet pan covered in aluminum foil or a wire rack placed over a sheet pan covered in aluminum foil.
3. Place the pan in a *cold* oven. Do *not* preheat the oven.
4. Turn the oven on to 400°F and set your timer to 20 minutes.
5. Check the bacon after 20 minutes to see whether it is done. The doneness will depend on how thickly the bacon has been cut and your personal preference.
6. If the bacon was cooked directly on the pan, you will need to transfer the bacon to a paper towel–lined plate to drain.
7. Enjoy!

Homemade Nut Milk

Makes 1 quart

2 cups raw unsalted organic nuts

4 cups filtered water

Pinch of finely ground sea salt (optional)

1 to 2 tablespoons local raw honey or other unrefined sweetener (optional)

1 teaspoon pure vanilla extract (optional)

1. Soak the nuts for the appropriate amount of time (see "Soaking Times for Nut Milk," page 33).
2. Discard the soaking water and rinse the nuts.
3. Place the soaked nuts in the filtered water, along with any optional ingredients, in a blender, pulse a few times to break up the nuts, then blend on high speed for 2 minutes.
4. Strain the nut milk through a nut milk bag, cheesecloth or other fine strainer and squeeze into a bowl.
5. Store in the refrigerator for up to five days. Shake the container before serving.

Homemade Coconut Milk

Similar to nut milks, coconut milk is a great alternative to dairy milk and is easy to make at home. There are two ways I recommend, depending on how it will be used. The first method is for coconut milk that is more drinkable. It is similar to what you find in a carton in a grocery store, but without all the added ingredients. This recipe makes a full quart. The second method creates the equivalent of one (13.5-ounce) can of full-fat coconut milk. This is a richer, fattier end product, but one that will work best in many of the recipes in this book. There are other ways to make coconut milk, but I find these two methods the fastest and easiest because you do not need fresh coconut and no soaking is required. For best results, use a high-speed blender.

METHOD #1

Makes 1 quart

2 cups unsweetened shredded coconut

4 cups filtered water (or use coconut water for an even more concentrated flavor)

1. Place the coconut and water in a high-speed blender and blend on high speed for 2 minutes.
2. Strain the mixture by pouring it into a nut milk bag, squeezing out the liquid, leaving the pulp behind in the bag.
3. Store the homemade coconut milk in the refrigerator for up to 5 days. Shake the container before serving.

METHOD #2

Makes the equivalent of 1 (13.5-ounce) can full-fat coconut milk

1½ cups unsweetened, finely shredded dried coconut

2½ cups boiling water (or boiling coconut water, for an even more concentrated flavor)

1. Place the coconut in a blender, add the boiling water and blend on high speed for 5 minutes.
2. Allow the mixture to cool, then pour into a nut milk bag and squeeze out the liquid into a bowl, leaving the pulp behind in the bag.
3. Store the homemade coconut milk in the refrigerator for up to 5 days. Shake the container before serving.

NOTE: Keep in mind that canned coconut cream taken from a can of full-fat coconut milk is recommended when making Whipped Coconut Cream (page 205) because it contains thickeners (usually guar gum) that allow the fat to be whipped into something similar to dairy whipped cream. Without that ingredient, you will not achieve the same result unless you add your own stabilizer, such as gelatin (see Stabilized Whipped Coconut Cream, page 206).

Homemade Ghee

Ghee can be used for searing meats, sautéing vegetables, cooking eggs or adding to sweeter recipes, such as many in this cookbook. The traditional way to make ghee is on the stovetop. By using the oven, you will avoid standing in front of the stove for long periods of time. It is important that the milk solids toast enough to imbue the ghee with a nutty taste, but if you let it go too far you can burn the solids and ruin the entire batch. The process is fairly simple and will result in a nicely toasted ghee without the need for constant observation (times will vary if you make different quantities).

Makes about 1½ cups ghee

1 pound (4 sticks) unsalted, organic, pastured butter

1. Place the butter in a Dutch oven or other oven-safe pan.
2. Place the pan in the oven and heat, uncovered, at 250°F (no need to preheat the oven). Check on it at 45 minutes. The milk solids should be rising to the top.
3. Continue to bake for another 30 minutes. At this point, the water is boiling off and the milk solids are beginning to settle to the bottom of the pan and are browning.
4. Remove the pan from the oven (about 1 hour 15 minutes total time) and allow to cool slightly.
5. Strain through three layers of cheesecloth. You will be left with the pure butter oil—no water or milk solids, such as lactose and casein.
6. Pour the ghee into a clean glass jar that can accommodate at least 12 ounces.
7. Store the ghee in the glass container at room temperature for up to 6 months or in the refrigerator for up to 1 year.

Breakfast

Almond Raspberry Muffins

Muffins have become standard breakfast fare for those who crave sweets in the morning. These muffins use far less sugar than do regular muffins and can be served any time of day. They are made with blanched almond flour, tapioca flour and almond extract for a nice, robust, nutty flavor complemented by fresh raspberries baked right in for a surprising burst of fresh fruit flavor. The optional crumble topping is a perfect finishing touch for some added texture and sweetness.

Makes 12 muffins

MUFFINS

2 cups (200 g) blanched almond flour

½ cup (64 g) tapioca flour

½ teaspoon baking soda

¼ teaspoon finely ground sea salt

3 large eggs

⅓ cup pure maple syrup

⅓ cup liquefied virgin coconut oil, or ghee or unsalted pastured butter, melted, plus more for muffin tin (optional)

1 teaspoon almond extract

1 cup fresh raspberries

CRUMBLE TOPPING

¼ cup coconut sugar

1 tablespoon almond flour

1 tablespoon tapioca flour

1 tablespoon liquefied coconut oil

Pinch of salt

1. Make the muffins: Preheat the oven to 350°F. Grease a 12-cup muffin tin or line with paper liners. (Or use a silicone muffin pan or silicone liners, for better results.)

2. Weigh the flours and sift together with the baking soda and salt into a medium-size bowl.

3. Whisk together the eggs, maple syrup, oil and almond extract in another bowl.

4. Pour the dry ingredients into the wet ingredients and stir until well combined.

5. Gently stir the raspberries into the batter and spoon the mixture into the prepared muffin cups.

6. Make the crumble topping: Stir the crumble ingredients in a small bowl and sprinkle evenly over the batter.

7. Bake for 20 to 25 minutes, until slightly golden on top. Serve warm.

NOTE: For delicious blueberry muffins, use vanilla extract instead of almond, and swap the raspberries for fresh blueberries.

Cardamom Banana Bread

Adding cardamom to a banana bread recipe is such a simple thing, yet it somehow transforms it into something more sophisticated. Strangely enough, cardamom is very popular in India and Scandinavia, two vastly different parts of the world. Cardamom has a strong, unique taste and an intensely aromatic fragrance that's a perfect complement to the sweet, ester smell and taste of a banana. This recipe is moist and aromatic—perfect with coffee in the morning or tea in the afternoon.

Makes 1 (7½ x 3½-inch) loaf

2 cups (200 g) blanched almond flour

⅓ cup (38 g) coconut flour

2 teaspoons ground cardamom

1 teaspoon baking soda

½ teaspoon ground cinnamon

¼ teaspoon finely ground sea salt

¼ cup liquefied coconut oil, or ghee or unsalted pastured butter, melted

1 cup mashed ripe banana (about 2 bananas)

3 large eggs

¼ cup pure maple syrup

2 teaspoons pure vanilla extract

1. Preheat the oven to 325°F. Grease a 7½ x 3½-inch loaf pan and line with parchment paper with the long ends coming over the sides.
2. Weigh the flours and sift together with the cardamom, baking soda, cinnamon, and salt into a medium-size bowl.
3. Place the oil, banana, eggs, maple syrup, and vanilla in a large bowl and stir together, or place them in the bowl of a stand mixer and beat on low speed with the paddle attachment.
4. Add the dry ingredients in thirds to the wet ingredients, mixing after each addition, and mix until fully incorporated.
5. Pour into the prepared loaf pan and smooth the top.
6. Bake for 45 to 55 minutes. The banana bread is done when a toothpick inserted into the center comes out clean.
7. Remove the pan from the oven. Let the banana bread cool in the pan for several minutes, then loosen the short ends with a knife and use the parchment paper to lift the loaf from the pan. Transfer to a wire rack to continue cooling.
8. Store in the refrigerator.

Cinnamon Rolls

Cinnamon rolls are a traditional and highly popular breakfast dish. In fact, just saying the words *cinnamon rolls* around breakfast time usually elicits squeals of delight and a mad rush to the kitchen. Unfortunately, store-bought cinnamon rolls are loaded with ingredients that you probably want to avoid, such as bleached flour, soybean oil, high-fructose corn syrup and a host of chemical-sounding additives. These all-natural, Paleo cinnamon rolls combine the healthier ingredients you prefer with a taste your whole family can enjoy.

Makes 8 cinnamon rolls

CINNAMON ROLLS

2 cups (200 g) blanched almond flour

1 cup (128 g) tapioca flour, plus more for dusting

1 teaspoon ground cinnamon

½ teaspoon finely ground sea salt

¼ teaspoon baking soda

2 large eggs

⅓ cup coconut oil

2 tablespoons honey

FILLING

3 tablespoons coconut sugar or maple sugar

1 tablespoon ground cinnamon

2 tablespoons raisins (optional)

2 tablespoons chopped pecans (optional)

COCONUT BUTTER ICING

3 tablespoons coconut butter

2 tablespoons almond or coconut milk

1 tablespoon raw honey

1. Make the cinnamon rolls: Preheat the oven to 350°F. Line a sheet pan with a silicone mat or parchment paper.
2. Weigh the flours and sift together with the cinnamon, salt and baking soda into a medium-size bowl.
3. Place the eggs, oil and honey in another medium-size bowl and mix well.
4. Add the wet ingredients to the dry ingredients and mix well. Wrap the dough in plastic wrap and chill for 15 minutes.
5. Place the dough in between two pieces of parchment paper and use a rolling pin to roll the dough evenly into an 8 x 12-inch rectangle that is ⅛ to ¼ inch thick. Use a little extra tapioca flour to keep the dough from sticking too much. (For best results when rolling up the dough, take your time to create straight edges for your rectangle.)
6. Make the filling: Combine the filling ingredients in a small bowl. Sprinkle the filling mixture over the flattened dough, then carefully roll it up. Use the bottom parchment paper to assist in rolling the dough.
7. Use a serrated knife to cut the roll into eight pieces. Carefully place each roll, one cut side up, on the prepared pan.
8. Bake for about 20 minutes, until golden brown. Remove from the oven and leave on the lined pan.
9. Make the icing: In a small bowl, stir the icing ingredients until combined. Drizzle over the cinnamon rolls. Serve warm.

Crèpes

The first time I made crèpes, my younger son walked into the kitchen and said, "Awesome. Pancakes!" When I informed him that crèpes are a classic French recipe and *not* pancakes, he calmly pointed first at the pan, then to the stack of crèpes, and responded, "Sure looks like pancakes to me, Mom." And of course, he was right. Crèpes *are* a form of thin pancake that originated along the Atlantic coast of France. It's common to serve crèpes alone or with a variety of savory or sweet fillings. One of my fondest memories of being in Paris for the first time was buying a giant, freshly made crepe from a street vendor. My chosen filling was a combination of Nutella and bananas and I was in heaven. Now we can re-create the thrill at home with gluten- and grain-free crèpes and fill them with Chocolate Hazelnut Spread (page 198).

Makes 6 crèpes

½ cup (64 g) tapioca flour

1 tablespoon coconut flour

¼ teaspoon finely ground sea salt

4 large eggs

2 large egg whites

½ cup light coconut milk or almond milk

1 tablespoon honey

1. Weigh the flours and place in a blender or food processor with the salt, eggs and egg whites, milk, and honey. Pulse until fully incorporated and no lumps remain. (Alternatively, if mixing by hand, combine the flours and salt; then, in a separate bowl, whisk together the eggs, egg whites, milk and honey. Make a well in the center of the dry ingredients and slowly add the liquids.)

2. Heat an 8- to 10-inch crepe pan or skillet over medium-high heat. Add a small amount of oil to the pan and spread evenly, covering the bottom and sides of the pan.

3. Ladle about ⅓ cup of batter (depending on the size of your pan) and swirl the pan so the batter spreads thinly around and covers the bottom evenly.

4. Cook for about 45 seconds on the first side, or until the edges start to separate from the pan. Use a spatula to loosen and flip the crepe over. Cook on the second side for 15 seconds and turn out onto parchment paper or a plate.

5. Continue with the remaining batter, adding a little more oil to the pan if the crèpes begin to stick.

Cherry Clafoutis

Clafoutis is a classic dessert popularized in France in the nineteenth century. This lightly sweet, baked dish has a thick, flanlike batter and is traditionally made with cherries. There are numerous variations using other fruits, including plums, apples, pears, cranberries or blackberries. When other kinds of fruits are used, the dish is called a *flaugnarde*. The classic clafoutis is dusted with powdered sugar and served lukewarm, sometimes with cream. Unlike the classic version, this recipe uses rich coconut milk and coconut flour to create a dairy-free, grain-free and nut-free dish perfect for breakfast, brunch or a more formal dessert.

Serves 8 to 12

4 large organic, pastured eggs

1 (13.5-ounce) can full-fat coconut milk

⅓ cup pure maple syrup

1 tablespoon pure vanilla extract

¾ cup (84 g) coconut flour

1 teaspoon ground cinnamon

⅛ teaspoon finely ground sea salt

1 pound fresh cherries, pitted and sliced (about 2 cups)

Whipped Coconut Cream (page 205) or Greek yogurt (optional)

1. Preheat the oven to 350°F. Grease a deep pie dish.
2. In the bowl of a stand mixer, combine the eggs, coconut milk, maple syrup and vanilla.
3. Sift together the coconut flour, cinnamon and salt.
4. Add the dry ingredients to the wet ingredients and beat, on low speed with the whisk attachment, into a smooth batter, about the consistency of pancake batter.
5. Pour the batter into the prepared dish. Carefully sprinkle the cherry slices evenly over the batter.
6. Bake for 45 minutes. Remove from the oven and allow to set up and cool slightly. Serve warm. It is delicious with a side of Whipped Coconut Cream or Greek yogurt.

Crystallized Ginger Scones

When I hear the word *scone*, I immediately think of an idyllic setting in the English countryside. It's common to think of scones as an English version of the American biscuit, but that's not exactly accurate. A scone is a type of pastry similar to shortbread, but with a different fat-to-flour ratio. The single-serving cakes are typically made of grain flour with baking powder for leavening, and baked on shallow pans. They are often lightly sweetened or glazed. These Paleo scones substitute almond flour and coconut flour for grain flour, and are seasoned with chopped, candied ginger. For an extra-special taste sensation, drizzle pure ginger syrup over the top. Serve for breakfast or during afternoon tea time with hot Earl Grey tea.

Makes 8 scones

2 cups (200 g) blanched almond flour

¾ cup (84 g) coconut flour

1 teaspoon gluten-free baking powder

¼ teaspoon finely ground sea salt

⅓ cup pure maple syrup

¼ cup liquefied coconut oil, or ghee or unsalted pastured butter, melted

Zest of 1 lemon

½ teaspoon pure vanilla extract

4 ounces chopped crystallized ginger, diced, or raisins or dried currants

2 teaspoons maple or turbinado sugar, for topping (optional)

1. Preheat the oven to 400°F. Line a baking sheet with parchment paper or a silicone mat and set aside.

2. Weigh the flours and sift together with the baking powder and salt into a medium-size mixing bowl.

3. Add the maple syrup, coconut oil, lemon zest and vanilla and work them in with a spoon until the mixture is slightly crumbly. Stir in the ginger.

4. Transfer the dough to the prepared baking sheet and shape it into a ball. Gently press until the dough comes together. Press the dough into a disk about 8 inches in diameter and 1 inch thick. Slice the disk into eight equal wedges (no need to separate the wedges) and sprinkle with maple sugar, if using.

5. Bake the scones until they are golden brown on the outside but moist on the inside, 15 to 20 minutes.

6. Allow the scones to cool on the baking sheet for several minutes before using a spatula or a knife to pull them apart.

Easy Strawberry Banana Milkshake

Fresh strawberries and frozen bananas. Coconut milk...a touch of raw honey...a blender. A perfectly refreshing drink all year round. This is one of the few recipes where I opt for light coconut milk because the frozen banana is enough to create a creamy texture. But if you like your smoothies extra rich, you can always opt for the full-fat version. Kids and adults alike love this simple, dairy-free milkshake.

Makes about 32 ounces; serves 2 to 4

2 frozen bananas

2 cups fresh or frozen strawberries, hulled

1 (13.5-ounce) can light or full-fat coconut milk

2 tablespoons raw honey or vegan alternative (see page 27)

Place all the ingredients in a blender and blend until smooth and creamy. Serve immediately.

Fluffy Coconut Flour Pancakes

The good news is you can follow a strict Paleo diet and still enjoy awesome-tasting pancakes on occasion without exposing yourself to gluten or nuts. The bad news is … well, there *is* no bad news. The first thing to notice, besides how good they taste, is how similar the texture is to that of traditional pancakes. Because these are high in fiber and protein and lower in sugar, you will stay feeling full much longer than with traditional pancakes. Keeping the pancakes on the small side will make them easier to flip.

Serves 4

4 large eggs, at room temperature

1 cup coconut milk

2 teaspoons pure vanilla extract

1 tablespoon honey or coconut nectar

½ cup plus 1 tablespoon (63 g) coconut flour

1 teaspoon baking soda

½ teaspoon finely ground sea salt

¼ teaspoon ground cinnamon

Coconut nectar, honey, pure maple syrup, fruit compote or Meyer Lemon Curd (page 139), for serving

1. Preheat a large skillet or griddle over medium-low heat.

2. Beat the eggs in the bowl of a stand mixer, using the whisk attachment on low speed, until frothy. Mix in the coconut milk, vanilla and honey.

3. In a small bowl, whisk together the coconut flour, baking soda, salt and cinnamon.

4. Add half of the dry ingredients to the wet ingredients and beat on medium speed for about 30 seconds. Scrape down the sides of the bowl, then add the remaining dry mixture and beat at medium to medium-high speed for another minute or two, or until the coconut flour is completely mixed into the batter and has fully absorbed the liquid.

5. Grease the heated pan with coconut oil, using a heat-proof silicone brush to spread the oil evenly between each batch). Spoon the batter onto the pan to create pancakes that are 2 to 3 inches in diameter, using the back of the spoon to spread them out. (Keep them small for easier flipping.)

6. Cook for 2 to 3 minutes, or until the pancakes are bubbling and well set, then flip and cook for an additional 1 to 2 minutes. Adjust the heat as necessary.

7. Serve hot with your choice of accompaniment.

8. You can freeze the prepared pancakes and reheat them later.

Paleo Granola

Once you put aside the obvious reference to grains, there's just something about the word *granola* that sounds healthy! Maybe it's all those TV advertisements I remember from the 1980s, full of tanned, blond models eating bowls of the stuff while sitting beneath the shade of a giant redwood tree ... or maybe it's the images of happy, Swiss people yodeling away their days in the Alps, then returning home for a meal of muesli and honey? All I know is that granola tastes good, and Paleo granola tastes really good, without all the grains you might want to avoid. It's a crunchy, nutty and sweet snack that can be enjoyed all year long.

Makes 8 cups granola

1 cup raw almonds

1 cup raw cashews

½ cup pistachios

½ cup hazelnuts

½ cup unsweetened shredded coconut

½ cup raw pumpkin seeds

¼ cup raw sunflower seeds

¼ cup coconut oil

⅓ cup honey

1 teaspoon pure vanilla extract

1 teaspoon ground cinnamon

1 teaspoon finely ground sea salt

1 cup dried cherries, lightly chopped

1 tablespoon lemon or orange zest (optional)

1. Preheat the oven to 275°F. Line a baking sheet with parchment or a silicone mat.
2. Roughly chop the almonds, cashews, pistachios and hazelnuts. Combine the chopped nuts with the coconut and seeds and set aside.
3. Combine the coconut oil, honey, vanilla, cinnamon and salt in a small pan and heat over low heat until warm. Pour the warm liquid over the nut mixture and stir to coat.
4. Spread the granola mixture evenly onto the prepared baking sheet and bake for 45 minutes, or until lightly browned, stirring every 15 minutes.
5. Remove from the oven, stir in cherries and citrus zest, if using, and spread out evenly on the baking sheet. Allow to cool completely. Break into pieces and pack the granola into a sealed container. It will keep for about 2 weeks.

Paleo Breakfast Porridge

When our family started down the path of creating a better, more healthful future for ourselves, we began transitioning to a grain-free diet. This porridge recipe really helped us out during that time. Our original "grain-free cereal" was in a simpler form—just bananas (or plantains), coconut milk, almond meal and flax meal. It was born out of desperation—the desperation to make something that remotely resembled oatmeal or other types of hot cereal, to replace what we were losing. Since those early days, our Paleo porridge has turned into a more complex dish. We began adding spices and different types of toppings, for more variety. We typically eat it as a side dish with a source of protein, such as sausage or eggs. It's great with an addition of berries, unsweetened coconut flakes and nuts. The sweetness will vary, depending on the ripeness of the bananas you are using. The bananas provide enough sweetness for our taste but you have the option of drizzling a little maple syrup or raw honey on the porridge before serving.

Makes about 4 (1-cup) servings

2 ripe bananas, or 1 large, very ripe plantain, mashed

2 cups light or full-fat coconut milk, or 1 (13.5-ounce) can, plus extra water as needed

¾ cup almond meal or almond flour

¼ cup flax meal

1 teaspoon ground cinnamon

½ teaspoon ground ginger

⅛ teaspoon ground cloves

⅛ teaspoon ground nutmeg

⅛ teaspoon finely ground sea salt

Pure maple syrup or raw honey, for serving (optional)

Berries, unsweetened coconut flakes, nuts, seeds, etc., or Paleo Granola (page 58), for topping

1. Combine all the ingredients, except the maple syrup and toppings, in a medium-size saucepan and heat over medium-low heat to a slow simmer, stirring often, until thick and bubbly. The consistency will vary, depending on the type of coconut milk you use (I usually use light coconut milk). The mixture will seem thin at first but will thicken up quickly. It will continue to thicken after it is served, so you may need to add extra water or coconut milk.

2. Add the maple syrup, if using, and preferred toppings to taste. Serve warm.

Cookies

Texas Cowboy Cookies

Have I mentioned I'm from Texas? Well, y'all—I am! I have lived in the Northeast for many years, but I'm a native of the Lone Star State. You may have heard it said that down in Texas, we like things BIG. When it comes to food, that can mean BIG size, BIG taste, or both. These dairy-free, grain-free cookies definitely satisfy on both counts. These cookies are like a grain-free version of oatmeal raisin cookies. Serve as an after-school treat, or a before-bedtime snack with hot chocolate (and pajamas, of course!).

Makes 24 to 30 cookies

2 cups (200 g) blanched almond flour

½ teaspoon baking soda

½ teaspoon finely ground sea salt

½ teaspoon ground cinnamon

⅛ teaspoon ground nutmeg

½ cup palm shortening

1 cup coconut sugar

1 large egg

1 tablespoon pure vanilla extract

½ cup unsweetened shredded coconut

½ cup chopped pecans

½ cup raisins or dark chocolate mini chips

1. Preheat the oven to 350°F. Line a baking sheet with parchment paper or a silicone mat.

2. Weigh the almond flour and sift together with baking soda, salt, cinnamon and nutmeg into a medium-size bowl. Set aside.

3. In a stand mixer, using the paddle attachment on slow to medium speed, cream the shortening and coconut sugar together. Add the egg and vanilla and continue to mix.

4. Add the flour mixture to the wet ingredients and continue to mix, stopping to scrape down the sides of the bowl as necessary, until combined. Stir in the coconut, pecans and raisins, or chocolate mini chips.

5. Use a small cookie dough scoop (1½ tablespoons) or form into 1½- to 2-inch balls and place about 3 inches apart on the prepared baking sheet. Press the dough balls to form disks about ¼ inch thick. (The dough does not automatically melt and spread out as much as with regular flour.)

6. Bake for 10 to 12 minutes. Transfer to a wire rack to cool.

FOR SLICE-AND-BAKE COOKIES

1. Prepare the dough according to steps 2 through 4, then turn out the dough onto a sheet of parchment paper and shape into one or two logs (whichever fits in a resealable plastic freezer bag or a freezer-safe container). Use the parchment to help roll the dough into a smooth log.

2. Wrap each of the logs in waxed paper and tuck in the ends.

3. Transfer the logs of dough to the bag or container. Press out as much air as possible, label the bag or container, and store in the freezer for up to 3 months.

4. When ready to bake the cookies, preheat the oven to 350°F and line a baking sheet with parchment paper or a silicone mat. Unwrap the log of cookie dough and let it rest at room temperature for 10 to 15 minutes. Slice the cookies into thick disks, using a very sharp chef's knife or serrated bread knife. Space the cookies a few inches apart on the prepared baking sheet and bake for 10 to 12 minutes. You may need to add an extra minute or so due to the coldness of the dough. Transfer to a wire rack to cool.

Best Ever Chocolate Chip Cookies

I f I only had one reason to keep blanched almond flour on hand, it would be to make these chocolate chip cookies. A similar version has been on my food blog, *Paleo Spirit*, for years and I have received dozens of comments extolling the virtues of these cookies. People love them because they are easy to make and taste exactly like classic chocolate chip cookies—if not better. And amazingly, the recipe is not only Paleo but egg free, too. That means you can feel free to eat the raw cookie dough to your heart's content without fear—not that I would know anything about that . . .

Makes 24 to 26 cookies

2 cups (200 g) blanched almond flour

2 tablespoons (14 g) coconut flour

½ teaspoon baking soda

½ teaspoon finely ground sea salt

1 tablespoon pure vanilla extract

½ cup liquefied virgin coconut oil, or ghee or unsalted pastured butter, melted

½ cup coconut nectar or pure maple syrup

¾ cup dark chocolate chips

1. Preheat the oven to 350°F. Line a baking sheet with parchment paper or a silicone mat.

2. Weigh the almond flour and sift together with the coconut flour, baking soda and salt into a large bowl.

3. Combine the vanilla, coconut oil and coconut nectar in a small bowl.

4. Stir the wet ingredients into the dry ingredients, and pour in the chocolate chips. Cover the batter and refrigerate for at least 30 minutes.

5. Use a small cookie dough scoop (1½ tablespoons) or form into 1½-inch balls and place at least 2 inches apart on the prepared baking sheet.

6. Bake 10 minutes, or a little longer if you like a crunchier cookie. Transfer to a wire rack to cool.

Gingerbread Men Cookies

In the classic children's story, a lonely little old woman and her equally lonely husband make themselves a boy out of gingerbread. As soon as the boy is finished cooking, he jumps out of the oven and runs away, chanting, "Run, run, as fast as you can! You can't catch me! I'm the gingerbread man!" while the whole town chases after him. His story ends badly, however, as the diminutive, snarky little pastry is eventually eaten by a clever fox. These gingerbread men might team up to plot their escape, but they'll probably be eaten quickly, too. But not by a fox.

Makes about 12 (5-inch) cookies

3 cups (300 g) blanched almond flour

2 tablespoons (16 g) arrowroot flour, plus more for rolling

1 teaspoon ground ginger

1 teaspoon ground cinnamon

½ teaspoon ground nutmeg

½ teaspoon baking soda

½ teaspoon finely ground sea salt

¼ teaspoon ground cloves

½ cup molasses

¼ cup pure maple syrup

3 tablespoons coconut oil

1 tablespoon light or full-fat coconut or almond milk

1. Preheat the oven to 350°F. Line a baking sheet with parchment paper or a silicone mat.

2. In a medium-size bowl, combine all the dry ingredients.

3. In a saucepan, combine the molasses, maple syrup, coconut oil and coconut milk and heat on low heat, stirring, until warm.

4. Pour the wet ingredients into the dry ingredients and mix well.

5. Form the dough into a disk, wrap in plastic wrap, and refrigerate for 10 to 15 minutes.

6. Roll out the dough between two sheets of parchment paper until about ¼ inch thick. (Sprinkle some arrowroot flour on the parchment paper as needed.) Cut the batter with your choice of cookie cutters and place about an inch apart on the prepared baking sheet.

7. Bake for 10 minutes. Transfer to a wire rack to cool, then decorate and serve.

Linzer Cookies

Whenever I see Linzer cookies, with their beautiful splash of red jam in the center, I feel as if I should be wearing white gloves and a tiara. These delicate, dairy-free delights are great after dinner as an attractive and delicious dessert. But my favorite way to serve Linzer cookies is at our traditional afterschool tea time with my two boys. The sprinkle of confectioners' sugar is definitely not Paleo, but is optional when serving on a special occasion.

Makes 12 to 15 cookies

2 cups (200 g) blanched almond flour

2 tablespoons (16 g) tapioca flour

¼ teaspoon finely ground sea salt

1 tablespoon liquefied coconut oil, ghee or unsalted pastured butter

1 large egg yolk

¼ cup honey

½ teaspoon pure vanilla extract

Fruit-sweetened jelly or jam of choice

Confectioners' sugar (optional)

1. Preheat the oven to 325°F.

2. Weigh the flours and sift together with the salt into a medium-size bowl.

3. Add the coconut oil, egg yolk , honey and vanilla to the flour mixture and stir well until combined into a dough. (You can use a food processor for this.)

4. Form the dough into a disk, wrap in plastic wrap, and refrigerate until firm—about 20 minutes

5. Roll out the dough between two pieces of parchment paper to about ⅛-inch thick and use Linzer cookie cutters to cut out the cookie shapes. (If you don't have Linzer cutters, cut pairs of dough disks and then use a mini cutter to create a decorative opening in the center of one of the disks.) Roll out the remaining dough again and continue to cut cookie shapes until you have used up all the dough. You should end up with 24 to 30 total cookie pieces, or 12 to 15 pairs of uncut and cut-out disks. Transfer carefully to the prepared baking sheet, leaving about an inch between the disks.

6. Bake for 7 to 9 minutes, then transfer to a wire rack to cool.

7. Spoon 1 teaspoon of jam onto each solid cookie, then top with the cut-out cookie to create a cookie sandwich.

8. Sprinkle the tops with a little bit of confectioners' sugar just for decoration, if desired.

Chocolate Shortbread Cookies

Shortbread is normally made with butter, which causes the well-known crumbly texture. Chemically speaking, the butter creates the crumbliness by preventing the formation of long protein strands. However, the fat content does not have to come from butter. In these cookies, it comes from coconut oil. Add cocoa powder, plus maple sugar for sweetness, and the result is the same crumbly texture you'd expect from shortbread, with the added delight of chocolate. Eat these cookies alone or use them to make ice cream sandwiches (see photo, page 165).

Makes about 4 dozen cookies

2 cups (200 g) blanched almond flour

¾ cup maple sugar

¼ cup unsweetened cocoa powder

3 tablespoons coconut flour

2 tablespoons tapioca flour

½ teaspoon finely ground sea salt

½ cup cold coconut oil, ghee or unsalted pastured butter

1. Preheat the oven to 350°F. Line a baking sheet with parchment paper or a silicone mat.

2. Using a food processor or pastry cutter, mix the almond flour, maple sugar, cocoa powder, coconut flour, tapioca flour and salt until combined. Cut the cold coconut oil into the dry mixture until the size of small peas.

3. Form the dough into a disk, cover in plastic wrap and refrigerate for 30 minutes.

4. Remove the shortbread dough from the refrigerator and roll out between two pieces of parchment paper to ⅛- to ¼-inch thickness.

5. Cut into your desired shapes and carefully transfer to the prepared baking sheet. (Using a spatula helps.)

6. Bake for 10 to 12 minutes. Remove from the oven and let cool on the pan, then transfer to a wire rack to cool completely once they have firmed up.

Vanilla Madeleines

The madeleine is a traditional small sponge cake with a distinctive shell-like shape that originated in the Alsace-Lorraine region of northeastern France. For hundreds of years, France and Germany fought numerous wars over the ownership of Alsace-Lorraine. It's yet to be determined whether control of the delicious madeleine played a role in these conflicts. However, fights may break out in your own home over who gets the last one in the cookie box! You can make this recipe with butter, which is classic, or use coconut oil if you prefer to remain dairy free.

Makes 12 madeleines

⅓ cup (38 g) coconut flour

¼ cup (32 g) arrowroot flour

⅛ teaspoon finely ground sea salt

½ cup coconut oil

2 large eggs, at room temperature

⅓ cup pure maple syrup

1 teaspoon orange or lemon zest

1 teaspoon fresh lemon juice

1 teaspoon pure vanilla extract

1. Preheat the oven to 350°F. Lightly oil a twelve-shell madeleine mold.

2. Weigh the flours and sift them together with the salt into a small mixing bowl.

3. In a medium-size mixing bowl, whisk together the remaining ingredients until well combined.

4. Add the wet ingredients to the dry ingredients and stir well until fully mixed.

5. Chill the dough for 30 minutes. *This is a very important step for the cookies to bake properly.*

6. Use a 1½-tablespoon cookie scoop to distribute the chilled dough equally among the prepared molds. You will use two scoops per mold. The dough should be chilled enough to maintain its round cookie-scoop shape.

7. Bake for 15 minutes. The dough will slowly melt, creating crispy browned edges and the classic "hump" in the middle. Let cool in the pan for a few minutes, until they can be transferred to a wire rack to continue cooling.

Chocolate Madeleines

Madeleines don't have to be one-size-fits-all. These madeleines offer the same moist, spongy sweetness you expect, but with the enticing taste of chocolate. They're great as an after-dinner treat or a stand-alone dessert. Top with just a sprinkling of confectioners' sugar to bring out the beautiful shell shape.

Makes 12 madeleines

⅓ cup (38 g) coconut flour

¼ cup (32 g) unsweetened cocoa powder

⅛ teaspoon finely ground sea salt

½ cup coconut oil

2 large eggs, at room temperature

½ cup pure maple syrup

2 teaspoons pure vanilla extract

1. Preheat the oven to 350°F. Lightly oil a twelve-shell madeleine mold.
2. Weigh the coconut and cocoa powder and sift together with the salt into a small mixing bowl.
3. In a medium-size mixing bowl, whisk together the remaining ingredients until well combined.
4. Add the wet ingredients to the dry ingredients and stir well until fully mixed.
5. Chill the dough for 30 minutes. *This is a very important step for the cookies to bake properly.*
6. Use a 1½-tablespoon cookie scoop to distribute the chilled dough equally among the prepared molds. You will use two scoops per mold. The dough should be chilled enough to maintain its round cookie-scoop shape.
7. Bake at 350°F for 15 minutes. The dough will slowly melt, creating crispy browned edges and the classic "hump" in the middle. Let cool in the pan for a few minutes, until they can be transferred to a wire rack to continue cooling.

Raspberry Coconut Macaroons

Macaroons were Paleo before Paleo was cool. These small, circular cookies are naturally gluten- and grain-free because they are made primarily of unsweetened coconut combined with egg whites. Maple sugar is an expensive ingredient, but if you were going to buy it for only one recipe, this would be it. The maple sugar gives just that little extra in terms of flavor that makes these macaroons over-the-top delicious. For an even more decadent treat, you can dip the cooked macaroons into melted dark chocolate.

Makes 24 to 30 macaroons

2⅔ cups (8 ounces [about 227 g]) unsweetened, finely shredded coconut

¾ cup maple sugar

2 tablespoons raw honey

2 teaspoons pure vanilla extract

2 large egg whites (about 66 g)

Generous pinch of finely ground sea salt

1 cup (6 ounces) fresh raspberries, washed and dried completely

6 ounces dark chocolate chips plus 1 teaspoon coconut oil, melted together (optional)

1. Preheat the oven to 325°F. Line a sheet pan with parchment or a silicone mat.

2. Place the coconut, maple sugar, honey, vanilla, egg whites and salt in the bowl of a stand mixer (or a large mixing bowl) and mix on low speed with a paddle attachment (or wooden spoon) until well combined. Do not overdo the mixing or break down the coconut too much.

3. Scrape down the sides of the mixing bowl and add the raspberries. Mix only until the batter is marbled throughout, leaving a few chunks of raspberries.

4. Using a 1½-tablespoon-size cookie scoop, scoop the mixture onto the prepared sheet, leaving an inch between scoops.

5. Bake for 30 to 35 minutes, or until the macaroons have turned a golden brown on top. I personally like when they are baked long enough to be crispy on the outside because it adds a nutty flavor that offsets the tartness of the raspberries and sweetness of the honey and maple sugar. But don't bake them for too long or they will dry out too much.

6. Allow the macaroons to cool completely on the pan and store in an airtight container. They will soften significantly over time, so for the best texture they are best served the same day they are made. The uncooked batter keeps well in the refrigerator, in a covered container, until ready to use.

7. For a dark chocolate coating on the bottom, dip the bottoms of the macaroons into the optional chocolate mixture. Place the chocolate-dipped macaroons onto a sheet pan that has been lined with waxed paper. Allow the chocolate to harden before serving. You can place the dipped macaroons in the refrigerator for a few minutes to speed up the process.

Meringue Kiss Cookies

These airy, puffy treats are simple to make and easy to enjoy. I combined egg whites and maple sugar to create these meringue "kisses." I like to sandwich them with the Chocolate Hazelnut Spread (page 198) for an extra nutty flavor and creamy texture that complements the crunch of the meringue kisses. Both the kisses and kiss cookie sandwiches are great served alone or with coffee or espresso.

Makes 35 to 45 kisses

2 large egg whites

⅓ cup maple sugar

¼ teaspoon cream of tartar

Pinch of finely ground sea salt

½ teaspoon pure vanilla extract

Chocolate Hazelnut Spread (page 198) or Chocolate Ganache (page 207; leave out the bacon), for filling (optional)

1. Preheat the oven to 200°F. Line two baking sheets with parchment paper or silicone mats.

2. Place the egg whites, maple sugar, cream of tartar, salt and vanilla in a heatproof bowl over a pot of simmering water. Constantly whisk the egg whites until the sugar has dissolved.

3. Remove the bowl from the pot. Using a whisk attachment on a stand mixer or a handheld mixer, slowly beat the egg mixture. Gradually increase the speed and continue to beat until stiff peaks have almost formed. The meringue is ready when the whisk attachment dipped into mixture leaves a curled but stiff peak when removed.

4. Transfer the mixture to a pastry bag fitted with a star tip and pipe ½- to ¾-inch-wide cookies, 1 inch apart, onto the prepared baking sheets.

5. Bake for 1½ hours (2 hours for larger meringues), then turn off the oven and allow the meringues to cool down with the oven door closed—2 to 3 hours should be enough but overnight is great, too.

6. Store the meringue cookies in an airtight container away from any heat or moisture. Alternatively, store them in the freezer; they can be enjoyed straight from the freezer without being thawed.

7. For a more decadent and impressive treat, sandwich two kisses with the Chocolate Hazelnut Spread. For a nut-free kiss, you can use the Chocolate Ganache as a filling.

Cantuccini with Vin Santo

Cantuccini are almond biscuits popular in Italy, and commonly referred to as biscotti. Vin Santo (holy wine) is an Italian dessert wine originating from Tuscany and made from dried, white grapes. When served together, the cantuccini are often dipped into the Vin Santo to absorb the flavor and prevent crumbling. I once carted a bottle of Vin Santo all the way home from Italy and hosted a dinner party for my family where I served authentic Tuscan food—including cantuccini dipped in Vin Santo. My teetotaling Great-Aunt Ann never let me forget that she hurt her jaw biting into one. I argued that would not have happened if she had dipped them in the Vin Santo as instructed! These cantuccini use almond flour for a gluten- and grain-free cookie that is crunchy but not hard enough to break your jaw. But I recommend dipping just to be sure. (For vegan biscotti, try the Double Chocolate Pistachio Biscotti, page 84.)

Makes 10 to 12 biscotti

1½ cups (150 g) blanched almond flour

½ cup (56 g) coconut flour

¼ cup (32 g) arrowroot flour

⅛ teaspoon finely ground sea salt

½ cup pure maple syrup

1 large egg, beaten

1 teaspoon almond extract

½ teaspoon anise extract (optional)

⅔ cup whole unsalted roasted or raw almonds

⅓ cup dried currants (optional)

1. Preheat the oven to 325°F. Line a baking sheet with parchment paper or a silicone mat.

2. Weigh the flours and sift together with the salt into a large bowl.

3. Stir in the maple syrup, beaten egg, almond extract and anise extract, if using. Work in the almonds and currants with a spoon.

4. Form the dough into a smooth 8 x 4-inch log on the prepared baking sheet.

5. Bake for 30 minutes, remove the pan from the oven and turn off the heat, then allow the dough log to cool completely—at least 1 hour—on the pan. At the half-hour point while the log cools, reheat the oven to 350°F.

6. Cut the dough log into ½-inch slices on the diagonal, using a sharp bread knife. Place the slices on their sides on the baking sheet and bake for 15 minutes more.

7. Allow the biscotti to cool briefly on the pan and then transfer to a wire rack to cool completely before serving. They should be fairly crispy.

8. Serve with a sweet dessert wine, such as Vin Santo.

Double Chocolate Pistachio Biscotti

The word for this unique cookie comes from the Italian root words *bis*, meaning "twice" and *cotto*, meaning "cooked." Versions of these twice-baked cookies have been used over the centuries as nonperishable food items for travelers. Our use for biscotti is less utilitarian and more about taste and pleasure. These rich chocolate biscotti have the added benefit of being vegan-friendly.

Makes 10 to 12 biscotti

1½ cups (150 g) blanched almond flour

¼ cup (28 g) coconut flour

¼ cup (32 g) unsweetened cocoa powder

½ teaspoon baking soda

¼ teaspoon finely ground sea salt

½ cup pure maple syrup

½ cup unsalted pistachios

½ cup dark chocolate chips

1. Preheat the oven to 350°F. Line a baking sheet with parchment paper or a silicone mat.

2. Weigh the flours and cocoa powder and sift together with baking soda and salt into a large bowl.

3. Stir in the maple syrup. Work in the pistachios and chocolate chips with a spoon.

4. Form the dough into an 8 x 4-inch log on the prepared baking sheet.

5. Bake for 30 minutes, remove the pan from the oven and turn off the heat, then allow the dough log to cool completely—at least 1 hour—on the pan. At the half-hour point while the log cools, reheat the oven to 350°F.

6. Carefully cut the dough log into ½-inch slices on the diagonal, using a sharp bread knife. Place the slices on their sides on the baking sheet and bake for 15 minutes more.

7. Allow the biscotti to cool completely on the pan before serving. They should be fairly crispy.

Cakes, Bars & Donuts

Paleo Chocolate Birthday Cake

This cake is the most popular recipe on *Paleo Spirit*. On several occasions after stressful days in the office, I have opened my e-mail to find letters from people raving about this gluten-free, grain-free, refined sugar-free and nut-free cake. Bringing a tear of joy to my eyes are those messages accompanied by adorable photos of babies' first birthday parties. People really appreciate being able to serve a delicious cake at special occasions without worrying that their guests will be unable to eat it due to gluten or nut allergies. Whether you are looking for the perfect, allergy-friendly cake for kids or simply enjoy a rich, dense and moist cake with a great crumb, this recipe is for you. We like to keep the cake on the smaller side, so I have provided two versions: (1) a 5-inch two-layer cake (that can be made into four layers by cutting each layer in half horizontally); and (2) an 8-inch two-layer cake. To frost, you could choose from among any number of frosting recipes, like my Honey Coconut Frosting (page 210).

Makes 1 (5-inch) or (8-inch) two-layer cake

FOR 2 (5-INCH) LAYERS

⅔ cup plus 1 tablespoon (83 g) coconut flour

½ cup (64 g) high-quality cacao powder

½ teaspoon baking soda

½ teaspoon finely ground sea salt

6 large eggs, at room temperature

½ cup liquefied coconut oil, or ghee or unsalted pastured butter, melted

¾ cup pure maple syrup

½ cup brewed coffee or water

1 tablespoon pure vanilla extract

FOR 2 (8-INCH) LAYERS

1 cup plus 2 tablespoons (126 g) coconut flour

¾ cup (96 g) high-quality cacao powder

¾ teaspoon baking soda

¾ teaspoon finely ground sea salt

9 large eggs, at room temperature

¾ cup liquefied coconut oil, or ghee or unsalted pastured butter, melted

1 cup plus 2 tablespoons pure maple syrup

¾ cup brewed coffee or water

1½ tablespoons pure vanilla extract

1. Preheat the oven to 350°F.
2. Grease your choice of cake pans and line the bottoms with parchment paper.
3. Combine the coconut flour, cacao, baking soda and salt in a small bowl and set aside.
4. In the bowl of a stand mixer, using the whisk attachment, whisk the eggs on low to medium speed.
5. Add the oil, maple syrup, coffee and vanilla and continue to mix until combined.
6. Add the dry ingredients to the wet ingredients and mix on low speed until incorporated—about 30 seconds. Scrape down the sides of the mixing bowl (you may need to do this a couple of times) and then beat the cake batter on high speed for about 1 full minute so that the batter is fluffy.
7. Divide the batter between the two prepared cake pans. It will be thick. Spread evenly in the pans.
8. Bake for 25 minutes (for 5-inch pans) or 30 minutes (for 8-inch pans), or until a toothpick inserted into the center comes out clean.
9. Allow to cool in the pans on a wire rack for 10 to 15 minutes. Use a knife to loosen the sides of each layer from its pan and turn out onto the wire rack to cool completely.

TO CREATE A FOUR-LAYER CAKE (PICTURED)

Follow the recipe for the 5-inch two-layer cake. Once the layers have cooled completely, cut each layer in half lengthwise. Frost each layer with a modest amount of frosting so it does not slide. You can either finish with an overall covering of frosting or leave the sides bare to show off the layers. If you wish to tint the icing, try India Tree brand natural food colorings.

Chocolate Beet Pudding Cake

Beets are a contradiction. When pulled out of the ground, they look like unappetizing, dirty round lumps. But when you cut one open, the intense purple-red color is almost shockingly beautiful. Beets are very healthy and highly versatile; you can eat them in soups and salads, roasted, sautéed and fried … you can even use them in a cake! I used roasted beets for this recipe, and the result was a moist, reddish-brown cake that has a puddinglike texture when served warm. If you cannot wrap your mind around the notion of eating beets in a cake, feel free to substitute applesauce for a tamer, if less thrilling, snack cake. Frost with Chocolate Ganache and Bacon Frosting (page 207) (pictured, omitting the bacon), Whipped Coconut Cream (page 205), or Avocado Chocolate Frosting (page 193).

Makes 1 (8- to 9-inch) cake or 6 mini Bundt cakes

½ cup (56 g) coconut flour

¾ cup (90 g) unsweetened cocoa powder

1 teaspoon baking soda

½ teaspoon fine finely ground sea salt

10 large, moist Medjool dates, pitted

¾ cup apple juice

¾ cup chopped roasted beet (about 1 large beet, roasted until very soft)

4 large eggs, at room temperature

½ cup liquefied coconut oil, or ghee or unsalted pastured butter, melted

2 teaspoons pure vanilla extract

½ cup strong brewed coffee

1. Preheat the oven to 350°F. Grease an 8- or 9-inch round cake pan with coconut oil and line with parchment paper.
2. Weigh the coconut flour and cocoa powder and sift together with the baking soda and salt into a medium-size bowl; set aside.
3. Place the dates in a food processor and pulse until coarsely chopped. Slowly add the apple juice to moisten the mixture.
4. Add the beets and continue to pulse until pureed and combined with the dates. Process until the beet puree is completely smooth.
5. Transfer the beet puree to the bowl of a stand mixer, add the eggs, coconut oil, vanilla and coffee and mix on medium-low speed, using the whisk attachment, until well combined.
6. Slowly add the dry ingredients to the wet ingredients and mix on low speed, scraping down the sides of the bowl, until you have a smooth batter.
7. Pour the batter into the prepared pan and smooth it with the back of a spatula.
8. Bake for 30 to 35 minutes (depending on pan size), or until a toothpick inserted into the center of the cake comes out clean.

TO MAKE MINI BUNDT CAKES (PICTURED)

Grease mini Bundt pans and bake for 20 to 28 minutes, depending on the size of the pans, or until a toothpick inserted into the center of a cake comes out clean.

Paleo Cranberry Bars

Cranberry Bliss Bars are a favorite seasonal treat at Starbucks. Every year they beckon to me from behind the glass of the pastry counter. Unfortunately, those delectable-looking morsels are *not* gluten-free so I have not been able to indulge my fantasy. However, the Starbucks version was the inspiration for these gluten-free, grain-free, dairy-free, dressed-up blondies. Compared to the original Starbucks bars, this version contains far less sugar and still manages to be moist and delicious.

Makes 8 large or 16 small servings

CAKE

2 cups (200 g) almond flour

1 tablespoon (7 g) coconut flour

1½ teaspoons ground ginger

¼ teaspoon baking soda

¼ teaspoon finely ground sea salt

1 cup granulated coconut sugar (or maple sugar, for a lighter color)

2 large eggs, at room temperature

1 teaspoon lemon or orange extract

½ cup liquefied coconut oil, or ghee or unsalted pastured butter, melted

¼ cup fruit-sweetened, dried cranberries

¼ cup white chocolate chips or chunks (optional)

FROSTING

½ cup palm shortening

2 tablespoons raw honey

1 tablespoon lemon or orange zest

2 teaspoons lemon or orange extract

¼ cup fruit-sweetened, dried cranberries

COCONUT BUTTER DRIZZLE #1

2 tablespoons coconut butter

2 teaspoons full-fat coconut milk

1½ teaspoons raw honey

¼ teaspoon lemon or orange extract

COCONUT BUTTER DRIZZLE #2

¼ cup white chocolate chips, melted together with ½ teaspoon coconut oil

1. To make the cake: Preheat the oven to 350°F. Grease an 8-inch square pan and place a layer of parchment paper in the bottom of the pan long enough to come up two opposite sides.

2. Weigh the flours and sift together with the ginger, baking soda and salt. Stir in the coconut sugar.

3. In a separate bowl, whisk the eggs, then whisk in the lemon extract and coconut oil.

4. Combine the wet ingredients with the dry ingredients and stir until thoroughly combined.

5. Stir in the cranberries and white chocolate chips, if using.

6. Pour into the prepared pan and smooth the top with a spatula.

7. Bake for 23 to 25 minutes. Remove from the oven and let cool completely in the pan on a wire rack. Lift out of the pan by using the sides of the parchment paper.

8. Make the frosting: Using an electric mixer, whip the shortening, honey, lemon zest and lemon extract together in a small bowl. Smooth the frosting over the cooled cake and top with the dried cranberries.

9. Mix together your choice of drizzle and drizzle over the frosted cake.

10. Cut the cake into quarters, then cut each square diagonally to get eight large triangles. For smaller servings, cut again to get sixteen pieces.

Almond Flour Vanilla Cupcakes

When I first started on this recipe, I thought to myself, "What could be easier than a simple, white vanilla cake, right?" Wrong! A Paleo vanilla cake needs to balance all of the qualities the name implies—taste, texture, moisture—but with distinctly Paleo ingredients that don't always behave. After several tries, I finally found the right combination of blanched almond flour and coconut flour to yield the desired results. The trick was to whip some of the egg whites separately and gently fold them into the batter before baking. This serves to make the batter airy and fluffy, just as a cake should be! I love to serve these cupcakes filled with Meyer Lemon Curd (page 139) and topped with Blueberry Buttercream (page 201), as in the photo.

Makes 12 cupcakes or 1 (8-inch) two-layer cake

Coconut oil, ghee, or unsalted pastured butter, for layer cake pans (optional)

2 cups (200 g) blanched almond flour

¼ cup (28 g) coconut flour

2 teaspoons baking soda

½ teaspoon finely ground sea salt

6 large eggs, at room temperature

½ teaspoon cream of tartar

½ cup pure maple syrup

½ cup liquefied coconut oil, or ghee or unsalted pastured butter, melted

2 tablespoons pure vanilla extract

1 tablespoon fresh lemon juice

1. Preheat the oven to 325°F. Line a twelve-cup muffin tin with paper liners or silicone cupcake molds. Alternatively, to make a layer cake, prepare two 8-inch round cake pans by oiling the bottoms and sides with coconut oil and placing a circular piece of parchment paper on the bottom of each pan to assist in easy removal.

2. Weigh the flours, then sift together along with the baking soda and salt into a medium-size bowl; set aside.

3. Break three of the eggs into a large mixing bowl. Separate the remaining three eggs, placing the yolks in the large mixing bowl with the other eggs. Place the remaining three egg whites in the bowl of a stand mixer on medium speed, and using the whisk attachment, beat with the cream of tartar until they form soft peaks.

4. To the bowl of eggs and yolks, add the maple syrup, coconut oil, vanilla and lemon juice and whisk together.

5. Add the dry mixture to the egg yolk mixture and stir until well combined.

6. Gently fold the whipped egg whites into the batter.

7. Divide the batter among the prepared muffin cups or cake pans.

8. Bake for 20 to 23 minutes (for the cupcakes), or until the centers are not soft and a toothpick inserted into the center comes out clean, or for about 30 minutes (for the cakes), or until a toothpick inserted into the center comes out clean.

9. Allow to cool for a few minutes in the pan, then turn out onto a wire rack to cool completely before frosting.

Angel Food Cake

Angel food cake is a sponge cake that originated in the USA around the turn of the twentieth century. Due to its light, fluffy texture, it was dubbed "food of the angels." Angel food cake uses a lot of egg whites—this recipe required twelve—whipped continuously until they stiffen. (You can save the egg yolks to make Chocolate or Vanilla Pastry Cream, page 136, or Meyer Lemon Curd, page 139.) Instead of traditional flour, I used a combination of arrowroot and coconut flours. Honey provides the sweetness in this light, spongy, heavenly cake. Drizzle with Simple Blackberry Sauce (page 190).

Makes 1 angel food cake

12 large egg whites (about 1½ cups)

1 cup (128 g) arrowroot flour

¼ cup (28 g) coconut flour

1 teaspoon baking soda

¼ teaspoon finely ground sea salt

1½ teaspoons cream of tartar

½ cup honey

2 teaspoons pure vanilla extract

½ teaspoon almond extract (optional)

1. Separate the egg whites into a large nonreactive metal or glass mixing bowl and let rest for about 30 minutes, until they come to room temperature.

2. Preheat the oven to 325°F. Have ready an ungreased 10-inch-diameter, 4-inch-deep tube pan with a removable bottom.

3. Weigh the flours and sift together with the baking soda and salt into a medium-size mixing bowl; set aside.

4. In the bowl of a stand mixer or using a hand mixer, beat together the egg whites and cream of tartar until soft peaks form.

5. Slowly add the honey, then the vanilla and almond extract, if using, beating until stiff peaks form. Do not overbeat.

6. Transfer the meringue to a very large, wide bowl.

7. Sift the flour mixture over the meringue, adding about a fourth at a time and gently folding it in while making sure to scrape the bottom of the bowl, until all the flour mixture is moistened. Do not overmix.

8. Spoon the mixture into the pan and smooth the top. Remove any air pockets by gently cutting through the center of the batter with a thin metal spatula or knife.

9. Bake for 30 to 35 minutes, or until a wooden skewer inserted into the center comes out dry and the cake springs back when touched.

10. Turn the cake upside down and cool for at least an hour in the pan. Most tube pans have legs to keep the top of the cake off the counter. If yours does not, invert onto a bottle inserted into the tube.

11. When cool, run your metal spatula or a knife around the sides to loosen. Remove the outer part of the pan. Run your spatula under the cake to loosen it from the bottom and transfer to a cake plate.

Apple Cider Donuts

This recipe is inspired by the amazing apple orchards found throughout my adopted state of New Jersey. Apple cider donuts are a traditional treat at farm stands, primarily in the autumn, and are usually served with piping-hot glasses of apple cider. These donuts are grain free, gluten free, dairy free and soy free, and contain only natural sugars, so they're a genuine Paleo treat that goes great with coffee at breakfast or as an after-school snack.

Makes 12 mini donuts

½ cup (56 g) coconut flour

½ teaspoon baking soda

½ teaspoon ground cinnamon

⅛ teaspoon finely ground sea salt

2 large eggs, at room temperature

2 tablespoons liquefied coconut oil

2 tablespoons honey

½ cup warm apple cider

CINNAMON-SUGAR COATING

2 tablespoons ghee or unsalted pastured butter, or liquefied coconut oil

½ cup granulated coconut sugar, or ¼ cup coconut sugar plus ¼ cup maple sugar

1 tablespoon ground cinnamon

1. Preheat a mini donut maker, or if using a standard oven, preheat the oven to 350°F and grease a standard donut pan.
2. In a small bowl, whisk together the coconut flour, baking soda, cinnamon and salt.
3. In a medium-size bowl, whisk together the eggs, oil and honey.
4. Add the dry ingredients to the wet ingredients and stir until combined.
5. Add the apple cider and mix until fully incorporated into the dough. Allow the dough to rest for about 3 minutes to ensure the moisture is absorbed by the coconut flour.
6. Scoop the donut batter into the preheated donut maker. (A cookie scooper makes it easy; use one that measures about 1½ tablespoons.)
7. Close the lid and cook for 2 to 3 minutes. If baking in an oven, bake in a prepared donut pan for 20 minutes. Remove from the oven and allow to cool for another 20 minutes before removing from the pan.
8. Carefully remove the cooked donuts from the pan.
9. Either brush the donuts with melted ghee or dip them in to cover both sides. Toss the donuts with the cinnamon-sugar mixture until coated.

Pecan Praline Cheesecake

Pecan pralines are another delicious memory from my younger years in Texas. My father, who was not known to spend much time cooking, was motivated to get in the kitchen a few times specifically to make pralines! Pralines are basically candy made from nuts and a creamy, sugary, caramelized coating. To mimic this distinctive flavor, I used honey to flavor a dairy-free cashew cream cheesecake on a date-sweetened, crushed-pecan crust and topped it with Whipped Coconut Cream (page 205) and toasted pecans. Drizzling Spiced Caramel Sauce (page 194) takes this dessert over the top in terms of taste and presentation.

Makes 1 (9-inch) cheesecake

CRUST

2 cups pecans, toasted (see note)

10 Medjool dates

½ cup unsweetened coconut flakes

Pinch of finely ground sea salt

CHEESECAKE FILLING

2 cups raw cashews, soaked in water for at least 4 hours or overnight, rinsed and drained

¾ cup apple cider, coconut milk or water

¼ cup cognac or preferred liqueur, or water

½ cup honey

½ cup liquefied coconut oil, or ghee, melted

2 teaspoons pure vanilla extract

Pinch of finely ground sea salt

¼ cup apple juice or water

2 teaspoons unflavored grass-fed gelatin or vegan equivalent (see page 27)

TOPPING

1 recipe Whipped Coconut Cream (page 205)

25 to 30 pecan halves, toasted, for topping (see note)

1. Lightly oil the sides of a 9-inch springform pan.
2. Make the crust: Combine the 2 cups of toasted pecans and the rest of the crust ingredients in a food processor and pulse until you get a coarse mixture. Pour into the prepared springform pan. Press down with your fingers or the back of a spoon to pack it evenly into the bottom of the pan to create a base.
3. Make the filling: Place the cashews in a food processor with the apple cider, cognac, honey, coconut oil, vanilla and salt and carefully pulse a few times until a paste begins to form. Stop to scrape down the sides a few times and continue to process for at least 10 minutes, until very smooth and creamy.
4. While the cashew mixture is processing, warm the apple juice in a small bowl, add the gelatin and stir until the gelatin melts completely. Immediately add the gelatin mixture to the cashew mixture and continue to process for another minute or two.
5. Pour the filling mixture into the springform pan on top of the tart base. Cover with plastic wrap and place in the refrigerator or freezer until set, at least 4 hours or overnight.
6. Remove the cake from the fridge or freezer. Prepare the Whipped Coconut Cream and spread evenly on top of the cake. Arrange the toasted pecan halves on top.

7. Before serving, allow the cheesecake to thaw slightly so you can remove the sides of the springform pan and so it can be cut.

NOTE: To toast the pecans, preheat the oven to 350°F. Spread the 2 cups of pecans (for the crust) and additional 25 to 30 pecan halves (for the topping) evenly on an ungreased sheet pan and toast in the preheated oven for about 7 minutes. Allow to cool, then divide as directed.

Spiced Harvest Cake

There's just something about carrot cake; most adults love it, but most kids … just don't. Until they taste it, at least. But getting them to taste it is often the biggest obstacle. That's why we decided to call this "Harvest Cake," instead. The name sounds less intimidating than "Carrot Cake," which can make vegetable-phobic individuals—like kids—break out in a cold sweat. Then, just to be devilish, we added apples and zucchini to the batter. The result is a moist, delicious, nut-free cake that will appeal to people of all ages, even kids. "Oh, you don't want to eat your vegetables, sweetie? That's okay! Here … have some Harvest Cake, instead!"

Frost with Italian Meringue Buttercream (page 209) or, if you can eat nuts, the Spiced Harvest Cake is also delicious covered in Maple Cashew Glaze (page 202). It mimics the richness of a cream cheese frosting without the dairy.

Makes 1 (8-inch) two-layer cake

1⅛ cups (140 g) coconut flour	6 large, moist Medjool dates, pitted
½ cup (64 g) arrowroot or tapioca flour	¾ cup pure maple syrup
2 teaspoons ground ginger	½ cup apple or orange juice
1 teaspoon ground cinnamon	6 large eggs
½ teaspoon ground allspice	½ cup liquefied coconut oil
½ teaspoon ground cardamom	1 tablespoon pure vanilla extract
¼ teaspoon ground nutmeg	1 cup grated carrot
¼ teaspoon ground cloves	1 cup grated zucchini
¾ teaspoon baking soda	1 cup cored, grated apple
¾ teaspoon finely ground sea salt	¼ teaspoon cream of tartar

1. Preheat the oven to 350°F. Use coconut oil to grease two 8-inch round cake pans and line the bottoms with parchment paper.
2. Weigh the flours and sift together with the spices, baking soda and salt into a medium-size bowl; set aside.
3. In a food processor or high-speed blender, puree the dates with the maple syrup and apple juice until you have a smooth paste, stopping to scrape down the sides as necessary.
4. Separate three of the eggs and place the egg whites in the bowl of a stand mixer. Allow them to come to room temperature.
5. In a separate large mixing bowl, place the three egg yolks along with the three remaining whole eggs, add the date puree, oil and vanilla and stir until combined.
6. Add the dry ingredients to the date mixture. Stir in the carrot, zucchini and apple.
7. In the stand mixer, using the whisk attachment on medium speed, whip the three egg whites until frothy. Add the cream of tartar and continue to whip until you have firm peaks.
8. Gently fold the whipped egg whites into the batter and continue folding until well combined, taking care not to overmix and lose the airiness of the eggs.
9. Divide the batter between the two prepared pans. It will be thick. Spread it out evenly.
10. Bake for about 30 minutes, or until a toothpick inserted into the center comes out clean. Allow the cake to cool for 10 minutes in the pan, then turn out onto a wire rack to continue cooling. Frost or glaze as desired when completely cool.

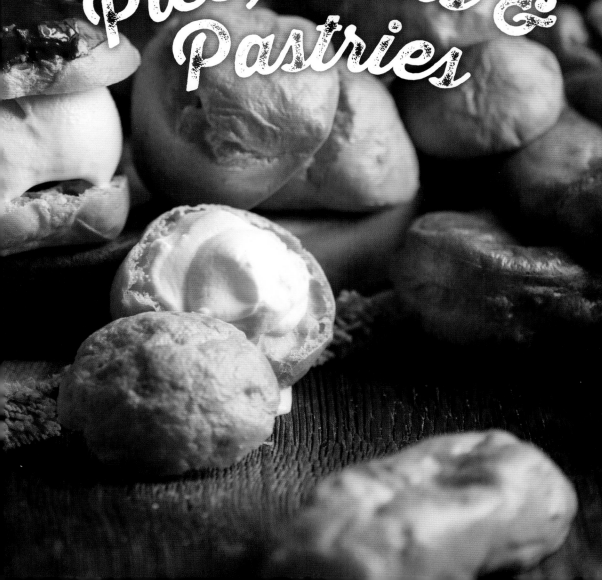

Pies, Tarts & Pastries

Almond Crumble

This sweet, buttery and crunchy crumble topping is a delicious addition to many different recipes. I like to use almond crumble as a layer in verrines, such as the Champagnne Sabayon and Almond Crumble Verrines on page 132. It's also wonderful as a topping for fruit that is then baked in the oven to create a simple fruit crumble dessert. Freeze the crumble mixture and save it until you are ready to use it as a topping on a fruit dish prior to baking.

Makes 3 cups crumble

1½ cups (150 g) almond flour or almond meal

¼ cup (32 g) arrowroot or tapioca flour

¾ cup maple sugar or coconut sugar

¼ teaspoon ground cinnamon

¼ teaspoon ground ginger

⅛ teaspoon finely ground sea salt

⅔ cup liquefied virgin coconut oil, or ghee or unsalted pastured butter, melted

¾ cup slivered, blanched almonds

1. Preheat the oven to 350°F.
2. Weigh the flours and sift them with the maple sugar, cinnamon, ginger, and salt into a large bowl. Add the oil and stir (or crumble the mixture with your hands, if necessary) to get it well combined.
3. Add the almonds and toss everything together. (If you will not be using the crumble right away, you can freeze it at this stage.)
4. Spread the crumble on an ungreased baking sheet and bake for 12 minutes, or until golden brown. Remove from the oven and allow to cool completely on the baking sheet. Alternatively, if you will be cooking the crumble on top of a dish that will then be baked—such as a fruit crumble—you can just put the mixture on the fruit in its unbaked state.
5. Store the crumble in an airtight container or freeze.

Sweet Tart Crust

This maple sugar–sweetened, gluten- and grain-free tart is extremely versatile. It is great for "no-bake" desserts and can be made ahead of time and then filled with custards, curds, chocolate mousse, fruit, whipped cream and more. It can be used as a standard-size pie or tart shell or as smaller tartlet shells.

Makes enough dough for one 9- to 9½-inch tart or pie shell

2 cups (200 g) blanched almond flour

3 tablespoons (21 g) coconut flour

½ cup maple sugar

½ teaspoon finely ground sea salt

¼ cup cold coconut oil, ghee, palm shortening, unsalted pastured butter or lard

1 large egg, beaten

1. Preheat the oven to 400°F.
2. Using a food processor or pastry cutter, mix the almond flour, coconut flour, maple sugar and salt until combined. Cut the cold oil into the flour mixture until the size of small peas.
3. Add the beaten egg and pulse just until a dough begins to form when you press it between two fingers.
4. Form the pastry into a ball, cover with plastic wrap and refrigerate for 30 minutes.
5. Remove the pastry dough from the fridge and press the dough into an ungreased 9- to 9½-inch tart pan. Prick the bottom of the dough all over with a fork, cover with parchment paper and weigh down, using dried beans or pie weights. Place the pan in the freezer for a few minutes if the dough has softened.
6. Bake for 13 to 15 minutes, or until the edges just begin to turn golden. Remove the beans and parchment paper and continue to bake for 3 to 5 minutes more, until the crust has completely turned golden brown. Remove from the oven and let cool.

Candied Blood Orange Tart

I first became acquainted with blood oranges during a study-abroad program in Italy while I was in college. Most of those oranges came from Sicily and were tangy and bursting with starkly red juice. Prior to that I had no idea such a beautiful thing existed. I was hooked. This tart recipe is an homage to that memory and combines honey-candied blood orange slices and a tangy, pink-tinted citrus filling inside a sweet tart crust. It is not only delicious but makes for a beautiful presentation no matter what pan shape you use. If you cannot find blood oranges, the recipe will work just fine with regular oranges. Serve with a side of Whipped Coconut Cream (page 205).

Makes 1 (13¾ x 4⅛-inch rectangular or 9½-inch round) tart

CANDIED BLOOD ORANGES

4 cups water

½ cup honey

4 smallish, thin-skinned blood oranges, cut into ⅛-inch-thick slices

BLOOD ORANGE CURD FILLING

¾ cup blood orange juice (at least 4 large oranges)

¼ cup lemon juice

1 tablespoon orange zest

⅔ cup pure maple syrup

1 large egg

5 large egg yolks

1 tablespoon tapioca flour

6 tablespoons ghee or unsalted pastured butter, melted, or liquefied coconut oil

1 teaspoon orange extract (optional)

⅛ teaspoon finely ground sea salt

TART SHELL

1 recipe Sweet Tart Crust (page 108)

1. Candy the blood oranges: Bring the water and honey to a boil in a medium-size pot.
2. Add the orange slices to the boiling honey mixture and lower the heat to a simmer. Cook for 45 minutes to an hour, or until the pith turns translucent, stirring carefully a few times to make sure to rotate the oranges from top to bottom so they are evenly candied. Be careful not to overcook the oranges or they will become too mushy.
3. Strain and remove the orange slices from the liquid. Lay out the orange slices on a wire mesh rack to drain and cool.
4. Make the filling: Whisk the orange juice, lemon juice, orange zest, maple syrup, egg, egg yolks and tapioca flour together in a medium-size, saucepan and slowly bring to a low boil. Simmer gently while stirring constantly until the curd is thickened and coats the sides of the pan and the spoon, about 10 minutes.
5. Remove the pan from the heat, add the ghee, orange extract and salt and stir until melted.
6. Run the filling through a fine-mesh sieve to remove the zest and any scrambled bits of egg.
7. Fill the tart shell with the warm filling and chill for a couple of hours until set. Decorate with the candied blood oranges.

Caramelized Banana Dessert Pizza

Maple sugar–caramelized bananas top this crispy, cinnamon-infused crust. Depending on your preference, you can slather the crust with different nut butters or spreads. Drizzle with Spiced Caramel Sauce (page 194) for a gluten-free, grain-free and dairy-free sweet pizza suitable as a breakfast side dish, snack or formal dessert.

Makes 1 (10- to 12-inch) dessert pizza

1 recipe Dessert Pizza Crust (page 127)

2 tablespoons maple sugar

1 teaspoon ground cinnamon

¼ cup almond butter, coconut butter or Chocolate Hazelnut Spread (page 198), or more to taste

2 to 3 bananas, sliced

2 to 4 tablespoons Spiced Caramel Sauce (page 194) or Coconut Butter Drizzle #1 (page 92)

2 tablespoons sliced almonds

1. Follow the directions on page 127 to create one Dessert Pizza Crust, slightly undercooking the crust because you will be broiling it after adding the toppings. Change the oven setting to broil.

2. Combine the maple sugar and cinnamon in a small bowl and set aside.

3. Cover the cooked pizza crust with the almond butter. Sprinkle with half of the maple sugar mixture and top with the sliced bananas, followed by the rest of the maple sugar mixture.

4. Broil in the oven for about 5 minutes, or until the maple sugar starts to caramelize, making sure not to burn the crust.

5. Finish the dessert pizza by drizzling with some Spiced Caramel Sauce, followed by a generous sprinkling of sliced almonds.

Meyer Lemon Meringue Pie

A billowy white cloud of meringue tops this lemon pie made with the extra-special flavor of Meyer lemons. If Meyer lemons are not available, feel free to use regular lemons. The recipe makes one pie or tart, but you can also make smaller tarts that make a beautiful presentation in individual servings.

Makes 1 (8-inch) pie or (9½-inch) tart, or several mini tarts

1 recipe Sweet Tart Crust (page 108)

1 recipe Meyer Lemon Curd (page 139)

1 cup filtered cold water

¼ cup (32 g) arrowroot flour

3 large egg whites, at room temperature

½ teaspoon cream of tartar

⅛ teaspoon finely ground sea salt

¼ cup honey

1 lemon, sliced thinly, for garnish

1 to 2 teaspoons lemon zest, for garnish

1. Prepare the crust by following the Sweet Tart Crust recipe, prebaking it in either in a 9½-inch tart pan or mini tart pans, preferably with removable bottoms, or an 8- or 9-inch pie pan. Allow the crust to cool completely.

2. Prepare the Meyer Lemon Curd through step 1. Whisk together the cold water and arrowroot flour and add to the lemon mixture along with the curd recipe's ghee in step 2, then continue as directed. Do not chill the curd; pour directly into the cooled crust and smooth the top. Refrigerate until chilled and set, 3 hours or up to 1 day.

3. Preheat the oven to 350°F.

4. Place the egg whites in the bowl of a stand mixer fitted with the whisk attachment and whisk on medium speed until frothy. Stop the mixer and sprinkle in the cream of tartar and salt. Continue to mix, gradually increasing the speed if necessary, until the egg whites form a meringue with soft peaks. Heat the honey until it is hot; then, with the mixer still running, slowly drizzle in the hot honey. Continue to beat until the meringue is glossy and is slightly cooled.

5. If you are making a standard pie or tart, you can simply pile the meringue on top of the pie, making sure it touches the crust all around.

6. If you are making smaller tarts, or if you want to get fancy with the meringue, place the meringue in a pastry bag with a large star tip and pipe the meringue onto the mini tarts, starting at the edge, making sure to touch the crust all around and piping from the outside in and spiraling up.

7. Bake until the meringue begins to brown, 8 to 10 minutes.

8. Garnish with the lemon slices and lemon zest. Serve at room temperature.

NOTE: For more tips on making meringue see "How to Make a Meringue" on page 31.

Chocolate Macaroon Crust

This multipurpose macaroon crust can be used with a number of different fillings, similar to the make-ahead Sweet Tart Crust recipe on page 108. You can make it into mini tarts or use it as a full-size tart or standard piecrust. One of the most exquisite ways to highlight the crust is to top it with Vanilla or Chocolate Pastry Cream (page 136) and fresh raspberries. And true chocolate lovers will swoon over this macaroon crust filled with Chocolate Hazelnut Spread (page 198). Great as an after-dinner treat with tea or coffee.

Makes enough macaroon for 1 (9-inch) tart crust or pie shell, or several tartlets

2 cups (160 g) unsweetened shredded coconut

⅓ cup coconut sugar or maple sugar

3.5 ounces (100 g) dark chocolate

2 tablespoons liquefied coconut oil, or ghee or unsalted pastured butter, melted

Pinch of finely ground sea salt

1 large egg white, at room temperature

1. Preheat the oven to 350°F. Prepare the pans(s) by greasing with a bit of oil.
2. Stir the shredded coconut and coconut sugar together in a medium-size bowl.
3. Melt the chocolate, coconut oil and salt together in a small bowl in the microwave, or using a double boiler, and stir until completely smooth.
4. Pour the melted chocolate onto the coconut mixture and stir until completely combined. Allow to cool.
5. Stir in the egg white until completely incorporated.
6. Press into the prepared pan(s).
7. Bake for about 15 minutes, or until the crust is crispy (time depends on which type of pan is used). If the crust puffs you can gently press it down while still warm. Let cool on a wire rack until room temperature.

Black Bottom Pecan Tart

For a delicious departure from standard pecan pie, I have created this tart that combines traditional flavors with chocolate and bourbon. The filling combines such flavors as maple syrup and molasses with the unique addition of pureed dates for extra sweetness and complexity. The texture is more akin to that of a firm tart than to a traditional gooey pecan pie, but you can make it in a standard pie pan as well. It is the perfect gluten- and grain-free addition to a holiday dessert table.

Makes 1 (9- to 9½-inch) tart

CRUST

¾ cup (84 g) coconut flour

½ cup pecans, toasted (see note)

½ cup cold unsalted pastured butter or coconut oil

2 tablespoons coconut sugar or maple sugar

¼ teaspoon finely ground sea salt

3 large eggs

FILLING

8 Medjool dates (or enough dates to make ½ cup puree), pitted and roughly chopped

½ cup pure maple syrup

3 large eggs

½ cup liquefied unsalted pastured butter or virgin coconut oil, at room temperature

1 tablespoon dark molasses

1 tablespoon bourbon (optional)

2 teaspoons pure vanilla extract

¼ teaspoon finely ground sea salt

1½ cups pecans, toasted (see note)

CHOCOLATE LAYER AND TOPPING

4 ounces dark chocolate

1 teaspoon coconut oil

⅓ cup pecan halves (about 25 pieces), toasted, for topping (see note)

1. Roughly chop 1½ cups of the toasted pecans in a food processor. Remove the chopped pecans from the food processor and reserve to use during assembly.

2. Prepare the crust: Weigh the coconut flour and pour into the food processor. Add ½ cup of the remaining unchopped, toasted pecans and the butter, coconut sugar and salt. Pulse until combined and the pecans are finely chopped. Add the eggs and pulse until a dough is formed.

3. Form the dough into a ball, wrap in plastic wrap and refrigerate for about 30 minutes.

4. Spread the dough evenly into the bottom and sides of an ungreased 9- to 9½-inch pie or tart pan. Chill for 30 minutes, during which the oven should be preheated to 350°F.

5. Prepare the filling: Place the dates in the food processor with the maple syrup. Process until the dates are completely pureed and you have a smooth mixture.

6. In the bowl of a stand mixer, place the date puree, eggs, butter, molasses, bourbon, if using, vanilla and salt and mix on medium speed until well combined. Set aside while you prepare the chocolate layer.

7. Make the chocolate layer: Melt the chocolate and coconut oil together and stir until smooth. Spoon onto the chilled tart crust and smooth over the crust until completely covered. Place the crust back into the refrigerator just long enough to harden the chocolate.

8. To assemble: Evenly layer the reserved chopped, toasted pecans into the bottom of the prepared tart shell. Pour the filling into the shell, over the chopped pecans. (You may have some filling left over.)

9. Decorate the top with the remaining ⅓ cup of unchopped, toasted pecan halves. Place the tart onto a sheet pan and bake for 35 to 45 minutes. Check the tart at 30 minutes.

10. Allow to cool on a wire rack.

NOTE: To toast the pecans, preheat the oven to 350°F. Spread the 2⅓ cups of pecan halves (2 cups for the crust and filling and additional ⅓ cup for the topping) evenly on an ungreased sheet pan and toast in the preheated oven for about 7 minutes. Allow to cool, then divide as directed.

Paleo Pie Crust

Grain-free pie crust dough can be harder to work with than standard dough because it lacks the gluten that provides the elasticity needed to roll out and transfer to a pie dish. I find the combination of flours in this recipe, along with very cold fat and one egg, will yield a dough that is fairly easy to roll out and assemble into a delicious and flaky pie crust.

Makes enough dough for one 9- to 9½-inch pie shell

1 cup (100 g) almond flour

½ cup (56 g) coconut flour

½ cup (64 g) arrowroot or tapioca flour, plus more for rolling out dough

½ teaspoon finely ground sea salt

½ cup (113 g) cold butter, palm shortening or lard (very cold)

1 egg

1 egg white plus 1 teaspoon water to make egg wash

1. Weigh and sift together the almond flour, coconut flour, tapioca flour and salt until combined.

2. Using a food processor or pastry cutter, cut the cold butter, palm shortening or lard into the flour mixture until the size of small peas.

3. Add the egg and pulse just until a dough begins to form.

4. Form the dough into a ball, flatten into a disk, cover with plastic wrap and refrigerate for 20 minutes.

5. Transfer the dough to a work surface covered with parchment paper that has been lightly floured with tapioca. Pat the dough into a ball and flatten it into a disk. Lightly dust the top of the disk with tapioca flour and use another sheet of parchment paper to cover the dough as you roll it out into a round at least 12 inches in diameter and about ⅛ inch thick. Continue sprinkling tapioca to ensure the dough doesn't stick to the paper.

6. Carefully transfer the rolled-out dough to your chosen pan using your fingers to repair any cracks.

7. Make an egg wash by whisking the egg white with a teaspoon of water. Brush the edges of dough with the egg wash. You also can use the egg wash to help adhere any decorative cutouts to the edges of the pie dough.

8. To partially or completely bake unfilled pastry, preheat the oven to 375 to 400°F. Bake for 15 to 18 minutes (10 to 12 minutes for partially baked shell). Let cool completely on a wire rack before filling.

TO MAKE A DOUBLE-CRUST PIE: Double the recipe, divide the dough into two equal balls and pat each half into a round, flat disk. Roll out one disk into a 12-inch round as directed and line the pie pan or dish. Combine any remaining scraps of dough with the second disk. Roll out the second dough disk into a round at least 12 inches in diameter and about ⅛ inch thick and refrigerate until ready to use. Use any remaining dough to create decorative cutouts.

Sweet Potato Pie

When I was growing up in Texas, our Thanksgiving and Christmas dessert tables almost always contained sweet potato pie. In fact, I'm not sure I ate pumpkin pie until much later in life—such is the tradition of sweet potato pies in the South. The addition of orange juice and zest in this recipe provides just the right brightness of flavor to the rich sweet potato custard filling. Top with Whipped Coconut Cream (page 205).

Makes one 9 to 9½ inch pie

2 large or 3 medium sweet potatoes

2 large eggs, beaten

½ cup full fat coconut milk

¾ cup coconut sugar

2 tablespoons butter or ghee, liquefied

1 tablespoon orange zest

1 tablespoon orange juice

1½ teaspoons vanilla extract

½ teaspoon ground nutmeg

¼ teaspoon finely ground sea salt

One uncooked Paleo Pie Crust (page 121)

2 tablespoons honey

PREPARE THE SWEET POTATO PUREE

1. Preheat the oven to 350°F.

2. Prick the sweet potatoes with a fork and roast them on a shallow baking pan until very tender, about 1 hour. Cool to room temperature.

3. Scoop the flesh from potatoes into a bowl and discard the skins. Mash the sweet potatoes with a fork until smooth. Measure out 2 cups of puree to use in this recipe.

MAKE THE SWEET POTATO PIE

1. Place a rimmed baking sheet on the lower rack of the oven. Preheat the oven to 350°F.

2. Combine the 2 cups mashed sweet potatoes with the remaining ingredients (except the pie crust) and beat with a whisk until smooth. (You may also use a stand mixer with whisk attachment)

3. Pour the filling into the prepared pie shell.

4. Carefully transfer the pie to the baking sheet set on the bottom rack of the oven and bake until the filling is just set, about 45 to 55 minutes. Transfer the pie to a rack to cool.

NOTE: To keep the crust from burning, I suggest using a pie shield or aluminum foil cutout to cover the outer crust. Cook the pie for about 10 minutes before adding the shield and keep an eye on it toward the end of cooking time to gauge whether or not you need to remove the shield for additional browning of the crust.

Pâte à Choux (Pastry Dough)

Pâte à choux (paht ah shoo) is a versatile classic French pastry dough made of flour, butter, eggs and water. The following recipe mimics the classic recipe with one big difference: It uses grain-free flours. These naturally gluten-free ingredients will create a product similar to the classic wheat-based pâte à choux recipe. Getting the quantity of eggs just right is tricky and the technique can take some practice. Once you master the pâte à choux recipe, you will be able to create small cream puff pastries and larger, round profiteroles.

When ready to serve, fill the pâte à choux pastries with Vanilla or Chocolate Pastry Cream (page 136), Basic Vanilla Bean Ice Cream (page 151), Whipped Coconut Cream (page 205) or another filling of choice. Consider topping with Simple Chocolate Sauce (page 214) or Maple Cashew Glaze (page 202).

Makes about 3 dozen cream puffs or 2 dozen profiteroles

1 cup (128 g) tapioca flour

¾ cup (75 g) finely ground, blanched almond flour

1 tablespoon (7 g) coconut flour

1 cup filtered water

½ cup (113 g) unsalted pastured butter, ghee or coconut oil

Pinch of finely ground sea salt

150 grams pastured egg (3 large eggs)

1. Weigh and sift together the flours and, set aside.

2. In a medium-size pot, bring the water, butter and salt to a simmer over medium heat. Add the flour mixture all at once, remove from the heat and stir very quickly with a wooden spoon or spatula to incorporate all the flour and form a sticky ball of dough. Return the pot to the heat and keep stirring while cooking off some of the water, another 2 to 3 minutes, or until the batter is drier and does not stick to the sides of the pan. (It will be an extremely sticky ball of paste.)

3. Transfer the paste to the bowl of a stand mixer fitted with the paddle attachment, or to a bowl if you are using a hand mixer, and mix on low speed for a few minutes, until the paste has cooled slightly.

4. Add the eggs one at a time, mixing rapidly until each is combined into the paste. The paste will go from shiny to slippery to sticky as the eggs are incorporated.

5. Preheat the oven to 425°F. Line a baking sheet with parchment paper or a silicone mat.

6. Spoon the dough into a pastry bag fitted with a large round tip. Pipe the pastry dough onto the prepared baking sheet, keeping the individual shapes about 2 inches apart because they will spread while baking. For cream puffs, pipe the pastry dough about an inch in diameter. For profiteroles, pipe about 2½ inches of dough into a round shape. For éclairs, you will want to pipe the dough into strips about 1 x 4 inches.

7. Bake at 425°F for 10 minutes, then turn down the heat to 350°F and continue baking for 18 to 30 minutes more, depending on the size of your pastry. Do *not* open the oven door during the baking process! Turn off the oven and leave the door cracked for a few minutes more to ensure the inside of the pastries will be dry enough. Times will vary.

8. Allow the baked pastries to cool completely on the pan. They will be very crunchy. Fill when completely cool.

NOTE: The pastries may also be frozen and thawed to room temperature before serving.

Profiteroles with Chocolate Sauce

Profiteroles are French pastries made of pâte à choux dough that is piped about 2½ inches in diameter to create a large puff pastry. The classic way to serve a profiterole is to fill it with pastry cream or ice cream and top it with chocolate sauce.

Makes about 2 dozen profiteroles

1 recipe Pâte à Choux pastry (page 124)
Basic Vanilla Bean Ice Cream (page 151)

Simple Chocolate Sauce (page 214)

Following the recipe for Pâte à Choux, pipe 2½-inch rounds of dough onto a baking sheet lined with parchment paper or a silicone mat. Bake according to the directions and allow to cool completely. Slice horizontally, fill with ice cream, and top with chocolate sauce.

Dessert Pizza Crust

My Paleo pizza crust recipe is one of the most popular recipes on my blog, *Paleo Spirit*. Time and again I get compliments from people amazed that a grain-free crust can taste so good and do a good job of replicating a standard, crispy pizza crust. I have changed a few of the ingredients to make this crust into a dessert crust suitable for sweeter applications. Use it to make Caramelized Banana Dessert Pizza on page 112.

Makes 1 (10- to 12-inch) dessert pizza crust

1 cup (128 g) tapioca or arrowroot flour, plus more for rolling

½ cup (56 g) plus up to 3 tablespoons (21 g) coconut flour, divided

2 tablespoons maple sugar

1 teaspoon ground cinnamon

¼ teaspoon finely ground sea salt

½ cup liquefied coconut oil

½ cup warm water

1 large egg, whisked

1. Preheat the oven to 450°F, heating a pizza stone if you have one.
2. Combine the tapioca flour, ½ cup of the coconut flour, and the maple sugar, cinnamon and salt in a medium-size bowl.
3. Pour in the coconut oil and warm water and stir.
4. Add the whisked egg and continue to mix until well combined.
5. Add 2 to 3 more tablespoons of coconut flour—1 tablespoon at a time—until the mixture is a soft but somewhat sticky dough.
6. Turn out the dough onto a surface sprinkled with tapioca flour and knead it gently until it is in a manageable ball that does not stick to your hands. (Add as much tapioca flour as you need, but be careful not to overwork the dough or add *too* much more tapioca, or your dough will be too dense and dry.)
7. Place the dough ball on a sheet of parchment paper. Cover with another layer of parchment paper and use a rolling pin to carefully roll out the dough until it is fairly thin. It should be 10 to 12 inches in diameter. (You may end up using another few tablespoons of tapioca at this point as well.)
8. Place the rolled-out dough—*including the parchment paper underneath*—on the hot pizza stone. Less optimally, place the dough, on its paper, on a sheet pan or the oven rack.
9. Bake for 12 to 15 minutes, depending on how "done" the crust should be before putting on your desired toppings.

Custards, Puddings & Mousses

Coconut Milk Panna Cotta

In Italian, the word *panna* means "cream" and *cotta* means "cooked." So *panna cotta* is literally "cooked cream." For a dairy-free option, we use coconut milk thickened with gelatin and flavored simply with vanilla. This dish is best served in a cup and topped with fresh berries or a fruit sauce, such as Roasted Strawberry Sauce (page 189) or Simple Blackberry Sauce (page 190).

Makes 6 (½-cup) servings

2 (13.5-ounce) cans full-fat coconut milk, divided

1 tablespoon unflavored grass-fed gelatin or vegan equivalent (see page 27)

⅓ cup raw honey

2 teaspoons pure vanilla extract

1 cup fresh berries or fruit sauce

1. Pour 1 cup of the coconut milk into a medium-size saucepan and sprinkle evenly with the gelatin. Let the mixture sit for a few minutes to allow the gelatin to soften.

2. Heat the coconut milk mixture over medium heat, stirring constantly, until the gelatin is dissolved and the mixture begins to steam. Stir in the remaining coconut milk and honey and whisk.

3. Remove the pan from the heat and stir in the vanilla. Let the mixture cool for 10 minutes.

4. Divide the panna cotta mixture evenly among six glasses or small bowls. Cover the dishes tightly with plastic wrap. Refrigerate for at least 4 hours, or until cold and set.

5. Top with seasonal berries to serve.

Champagne Sabayon and Almond Crumble Verrines

A verrine is a small glass container without a base. Desserts served in a verrine emphasize the vertical, and are usually prepared in three layers: a thin, lower layer to prime the taste buds; a middle layer to provide the main taste; and an upper layer of a smooth, silky substance that gives a sweet, memorable finish. The idea is to allow for a full appreciation of both visual and taste sensations. In this recipe, the lower layer consists of Almond Crumble (page 107), the middle layer is thinly sliced ripe strawberries or other fresh fruit, and the upper layer is a frothy Champagne Sabayon (page 213).

Makes 4 verrines

1 pint fresh strawberries or fruit of choice

1 cup Almond Crumble (page 107)

1 to 1½ cups Champagne Sabayon (page 213)

Fresh mint leaves, for garnish

1. Wash and dry the strawberries, remove the tops and slice lengthwise.
2. Place 2 tablespoons of the crumble on the bottom of each of four serving glasses. Top with sliced strawberries, followed by Champagne Sabayon, and finish with more of the crumble and fresh mint.
3. Serve immediately.

NOTE: The full recipes of Almond Crumble and Champagne Sabayon would yield at least double the amount you need here; if you choose to create more verrines, just add more fresh fruit.

Mexican Chocolate Mousse

Mexican chocolate combines the flavors of cinnamon, nutmeg and cayenne for a distinctive flavor often used in hot chocolate or espresso drinks. This chocolate mousse is a dairy-free version of a classic dessert, using coconut milk as the base and a bit of gelatin as a stabilizer. Top with a dollop of Whipped Coconut Cream (page 205) and a sprinkle of cinnamon.

Makes about 4 (½-cup) servings

1 (13.5-ounce) can full-fat coconut milk

¼ cup raw honey, or more to taste

1 teaspoon pure vanilla extract

2 teaspoons unflavored grass-fed gelatin

3 tablespoons unsweetened cocoa powder

1½ teaspoons ground cinnamon

¼ teaspoon ground nutmeg

⅛ teaspoon cayenne pepper, or to taste

Pinch of finely ground sea salt

1. Combine the coconut milk, honey and vanilla in a saucepan and heat until warm. Pour about ¼ cup of the warmed mixture into a small bowl and sprinkle evenly with the gelatin. Allow the gelatin to absorb the liquid and "bloom." You may need to give it a stir to combine completely.

2. Transfer the gelatin mixture to a blender, add the remaining ingredients and process for 1 to 2 minutes, until fully combined and frothy.

3. Immediately pour into serving cups, cover and refrigerate until set.

Pastry Cream

This pastry cream or custard is an extremely versatile recipe for a dairy-free option to fill pastries, pies, cakes and more. The coconut milk flavor is mellowed with the addition of vanilla bean seeds and vanilla extract. Try it with the Chocolate Macaroon Crust (page 116).

Makes about 4 cups pastry cream—enough to fill a 9-inch pie or tart crust

VANILLA PASTRY CREAM

2 cups coconut cream (the top cream layer of 2 to 3 cans chilled, full-fat coconut milk)

6 large egg yolks

⅔ cup (85 g) arrowroot flour

½ cup honey

1 tablespoon vanilla powder or pure vanilla extract

Seeds scraped from 1 vanilla bean

1. Whisk all the ingredients together in a medium-size saucepan and, whisking constantly, bring the mixture to almost a simmer over medium-low heat. Continue to cook until thickened, 5 to 10 minutes.

2. To remove any lumps, strain the custard through a fine-mesh sieve into a bowl or large measuring cup. Use a rubber spatula to press it through the sieve.

3. Cover the surface with plastic wrap to keep it from forming a skin. If you will be using the pastry cream right away, simply allow it to come to room temperature. Otherwise, refrigerate for up to 1 week. Remove it from the refrigerator about an hour before using.

CHOCOLATE PASTRY CREAM

For chocolate pastry cream, add 3 tablespoons unsweetened cocoa powder and follow instructions for Vanilla Pastry Cream.

Meyer Lemon Curd

Homemade lemon curd has been popular in England since the late nineteenth century. It is traditionally served with scones at afternoon tea as an alternative to jam. This classic spread is made with fruit juice, butter, eggs and sugar gently cooked together until thick then allowed to cool. Historically, curd has been made in small batches because it did not keep long. But nowadays, commercially manufactured curds often contain preservatives and thickening agents to make them more shelf-stable. Gourmet gift shops and food stores catering to epicurean tastes often stock curd, but you can make it yourself at home without all the additives. This recipe combines the traditional curd ingredients with the unique flavor of Meyer lemon juice, which is sweeter and mellower than regular lemon juice. I have used honey as a sweetener and swapped out the butter for ghee to keep it free from casein. The result is a smooth, creamy and rich, melt-in-the-mouth blend of flavors. It is the perfect filling for cakes, small pastries and tarts (see Almond Flour Vanilla Cupcakes, page 95, and Blueberry Buttercream, page 201). You can also use it as a spread on grain-free scones, such as the Crystallized Ginger Scones on page 53.

Makes about 1¾ cups lemon curd

6 large egg yolks

½ cup honey

½ cup Meyer lemon juice

1 tablespoon Meyer lemon zest

6 tablespoons ghee or unsalted pastured butter

1. Whisk the yolks, honey, juice, and zest together in a medium-size bowl over a simmering pot of water, until the curd is thickened and coats the sides of the bowl and the spoon, 15 to 20 minutes.

2. Remove the bowl from the pan, add the ghee and stir until melted.

3. Run the curd through a fine-mesh sieve to remove the zest and any scrambled bits of egg.

4. Pour into a jar and refrigerate. The curd will thicken as it cools.

5. Store the curd in the refrigerator for up to 1 week or freeze for up to 6 months.

Crème Brûlée

Crème brûlée (literally, "burnt cream") is one of my favorite desserts. Not only is it delicious, but it is one of the few items those of us who must remain gluten-free are able to order on a restaurant dessert menu. However, if you are dairy free, you don't really have that option. This recipe is completely dairy free, enabling those who are eating Paleo as well as those who need to remain dairy free the chance to enjoy a special treat they might normally have to avoid. Fresh berries are the perfect complement to this rich and creamy custard.

Makes 4 servings

Seeds scraped from ½ vanilla bean, pod reserved

2 cups coconut cream

5 large egg yolks

2 tablespoons honey

¼ cup maple sugar

1. Preheat the oven to 325°F. Place four ramekins on a baking pan, roasting pan or rimmed baking sheet.
2. Place the vanilla bean pod and seeds in a saucepan along with the coconut cream. Slowly warm the mixture over medium heat, whisking occasionally, just until foam begins to form around the edge.
3. In a bowl, whisk together the egg yolks and honey.
4. While continuing to whisk the yolk mixture, very gradually add about half the coconut cream mixture to the yolk mixture. This will temper the egg yolks. Return the tempered yolk mixture to the pan with the remaining coconut cream mixture and simmer, whisking, for about 2 minutes until somewhat thickened. Remove from the heat and allow to cool for a minute, then strain through a fine-mesh sieve.
5. Divide the custard mixture equally among the ramekins. Transfer the baking pan (with the filled ramekins) to the oven and pour enough hot water into the baking pan to come to halfway up the side of the ramekins. Bake until the custard is set but still a little jiggly in the center, anywhere from 30 to 45 minutes, depending on type of ramekin.
6. Remove from the oven and allow to cool. Cover with plastic wrap and refrigerate for at least 4 hours, or up to 3 days.
7. When ready to serve, evenly spread the maple sugar over the tops of custards. Using a torch or oven broiler, carefully melt the sugar until golden brown. You may also use an oven broiler but the sugar will brown less evenly and the custard can melt if it gets too hot.
8. Let cool until the sugar hardens and custard rests (20 to 30 minutes), and enjoy immediately!

Tiramisu

Tiramisu is a classic coffee-flavored Italian dessert. The name means "pick me up" in Italian, presumably because it is so enticing as to be impossible to resist. Tiramisu is made of ladyfinger cookies soaked in espresso and amaretto, covered with a layer of mascarpone cheese sabayon and dusted with unsweetened cocoa and espresso powders. Tiramisu is a rich and decadent treat, best served with a light dessert wine or a shot of hot espresso. This recipe uses full-fat dairy ingredients for an authentic experience. But for a completely dairy-free tiramisu—the ladyfingers and topping are already dairy free—you can substitute 2 cups of the Vanilla Pastry Cream (page 136) lightened up with one cup of the Whipped Coconut Cream (page 205) for the mascarpone filling, and proceed as directed.

Makes 1 tiramisu; 10 to 12 servings

LADYFINGERS (MAKES 24 LADYFINGERS)

6 large eggs, at room temperature

½ teaspoon cream of tartar

⅓ cup pure maple syrup

1½ teaspoons pure vanilla extract

⅛ teaspoon finely ground sea salt

½ cup (56 g) coconut flour

½ teaspoon baking soda

MASCARPONE CREAM

6 large egg yolks

¾ cup granulated maple sugar or coconut sugar

1 teaspoon pure vanilla extract

2 cups mascarpone cheese

ESPRESSO SYRUP AND TOPPING

½ cup cold brewed espresso

¼ cup amaretto or other almond-flavored liqueur (optional)

2 tablespoons unsweetened cocoa powder, for dusting

1 teaspoon espresso powder, for dusting

Dark or white chocolate shavings for garnish

1. Make the ladyfingers: Preheat the oven to 400°F. Line two cookie sheets with parchment paper or silicone mats.

2. Separate three of the eggs, placing the three egg whites in the bowl of a stand mixer and the three eggs yolks in a separate large bowl.

3. Using an electric mixer fitted with the whisk attachment, beat the three egg whites on medium-low speed until frothy. Add the cream of tartar and continue to beat until stiff peaks form.

4. To the bowl of yolks, add the three remaining eggs and the maple syrup, vanilla and salt. Whisk together until pale yellow.

5. Weigh the coconut flour and sift together with the baking soda into the large bowl. Add the egg yolk mixture and stir until well combined. Gently fold the egg whites into the batter just until combined.

6. Transfer the batter to a piping bag with a large round tip (or a resealable plastic bag with one bottom corner cut off) and pipe 3 x 1-inch strips onto the prepared pans. Leave 2 inches between the batter strips because they will spread.

7. Bake for 9 to 11 minutes, until just barely golden.

8. Allow the cookies to cool completely before removing from the sheet or assembling the tiramisu.

9. Make the mascarpone filling : Combine the egg yolks, maple sugar and vanilla in the top of a double boiler, or a heatproof bowl over a pot of boiling water. Cook for about 10 minutes, whisking constantly. Remove from the heat and allow to cool slightly. Cover and refrigerate for at least one hour.

10. Add the room-temperature mascarpone to the custard mixture and whisk until combined.

11. Make the espresso topping: Combine the cold espresso with the amaretto.

12. Assemble the tiramisu: Line a 9 x 5-inch loaf pan with plastic wrap. Dip one third of the ladyfingers in the espresso mixture, one at a time, and place them on the bottom of the pan in a single layer. Spread almost one third of the mascarpone filling over the ladyfingers. Place a second layer of espresso-dipped ladyfingers and spread another one third mascarpone filling on top. Dip the remining ladyfingers in the espresso and arrange them over the mascarpone filling. Spread the remaining mascarpone filling, cover tightly with plastic wrap and refrigerate for at least 4 hours or overnight.

13. Gently remove the tiramisu from the pan, and dust with cocoa powder and espresso powder. Sprinkle chocolate shavings before serving.

Grilled Apricots with Honeyed Almonds and Coconut Cream

Apricots make for a sweet, tart treat that goes really well as an accent to other dessert dishes, such as pie or ice cream, or on its own. This recipe uses heat to bring out the rich, tangy flavor of fresh apricots, and combines it with honeyed almonds and Whipped Coconut Cream (page 205) for a delicately balanced taste. Serve with breakfast or after dinner with coffee or an aperitif.

Makes 5 to 6 servings

½ cup slivered almonds

3 tablespoons honey, or more to taste, divided

10 to 12 fresh apricots, cut in half and pitted

Coconut oil, for brushing

1 cup Whipped Coconut Cream (page 205)

1. Preheat the oven to 350°F.
2. Spread out almonds on a sheet pan and bake for 5 to 7 minutes, until fragrant. Remove from the oven and mix with 1 tablespoon of the honey. Set aside.
3. Start with a clean, oiled grill or grill pan. Heat the grill to high. Brush the apricots with coconut oil on both sides and grill, cut side down, about 1½ minutes. Turn over and continue to grill for 1 minute. Transfer to a serving plate and drizzle with the remaining 2 tablespoons of honey.
4. Top with the honeyed almonds and Whipped Coconut Cream.

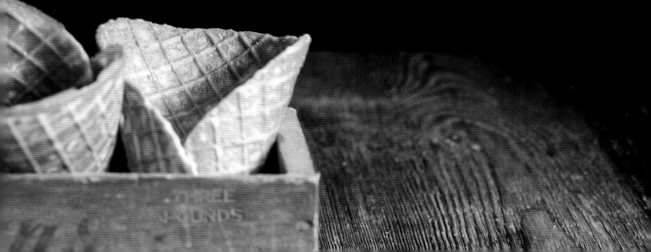

Frozen Treats

Basic Vanilla Bean Ice Cream

Vanilla is the most classic of all the ice cream flavors and can hold its own against the fanciest flavors out there. It is hard to beat the intensity imparted by adding high-quality vanilla beans to an ice cream base. This dairy-free recipe uses a combination of coconut and nut milks to lend a more neutral base that allows the vanilla bean taste to shine through. Dates and your choice of either maple syrup or raw honey sweeten the mixture. The date paste also helps thicken the ice cream, but so does an optional addition of gelatin for a rich, creamy end product. Use this Basic Vanilla Bean Ice Cream with the Tipsy Affogato al Caffè (page 168) or Gingerbread Men Ice Cream Sandwiches (page 171), or simply as a scoop in a bowl topped with Simple Chocolate Sauce (page 214).

Makes about 1 quart ice cream

1 (13.5-ounce) can full-fat coconut milk or 1⅔ cups homemade coconut milk (see "Homemade Coconut Milk," page 37)

⅓ cup pitted Medjool dates, roughly chopped (about 5 large, moist dates)

¼ cup pure maple syrup or raw honey

Seeds scraped from 1 vanilla bean

2 teaspoons pure vanilla extract (use 1 tablespoon if you are not using vanilla bean seeds)

Pinch of finely ground sea salt

2 teaspoons unflavored grass-fed gelatin or vegan alternative, plus ¼ cup boiling water, to thicken (optional)

1¼ cups unsweetened nut milk (see "Homemade Nut Milk," page 36)

1. Place the coconut milk, dates, maple syrup, vanilla seeds, vanilla extract and salt in a food processor or high-speed blender. Pulse a few times at first and then process the mixture for several minutes, scraping down the sides as necessary, until the dates are completely liquefied.

2. If you are using the gelatin: Pour the boiling water into a small bowl. Sprinkle the gelatin evenly on top and allow it to soften and absorb the liquid.

3. Add the bloomed gelatin, if using, and the nut milk to the coconut milk mixture and process until smooth.

4. Transfer the mixture to a 6-cup rectangular dish and refrigerate until chilled, about 2 hours, then pour into an ice cream maker and churn according to the manufacturer's directions. Eat the ice cream immediately or transfer to a freezer-safe container and freeze until firm.

Pistachio Ice Cream

Thankfully, the days when pistachios were dyed bright red are long gone. This recipe enhances the natural green color of the pistachio nut by combining it with avocado, which, when paired with coconut milk, gives it a rich, creamy consistency reminiscent of butter pecan ice cream. And if your family or friends don't like avocados, don't tell them; chances are they will never know.

Makes about 1 quart ice cream

1 cup shelled, roasted, unsalted pistachios

1 ripe avocado, peeled and pitted

1 (13.5-ounce) can full-fat coconut milk

½ cup pure maple syrup

1 teaspoon pure vanilla extract

Pinch of finely ground sea salt

1. Use a food processor or high-speed blender to grind the pistachios into a somewhat fine consistency—it's okay to leave a few larger pieces.

2. Add the remaining ingredients to the food processor and process until smooth and creamy.

3. Transfer to a bowl, cover and refrigerate until chilled, at least 2 hours. Process the chilled ice cream mixture in an ice cream maker according to the manufacturer's directions, 15 to 20 minutes, or until thick.

4. Transfer the ice cream to a freezer-safe container and freeze for at least 2 hours, or until firm enough to scoop.

Honey Yogurt Gelato

After living and working in Italy for nearly two years, I developed a deep fondness for what Americans like to call Italian ice cream, but what Italians know by the name *gelato* (juh-lah-toh). Although outwardly similar, there are differences. In contrast to American ice cream, gelato contains a relatively small amount of air, and is not frozen solid before serving. Handmade gelato is a huge industry in Italy, where high-quality goods of all types are appreciated. To this day, indulging in gelato brings back joyful memories of my time spent in that most wonderful of countries. If you're able to tolerate dairy and happen to have some high-quality Greek yogurt, then this honey yogurt gelato will not disappoint. You can vary the amount of honey depending on your taste preferences.

Makes 3½ cups gelato

2 cups unsweetened, organic, whole-milk Greek yogurt

1 cup organic, grass-fed buttermilk*

⅓ to ½ cup raw honey

1 tablespoon lemon juice

1. Whisk together all the ingredients until mixture is completely combined and smooth.
2. Cover and refrigerate for about an hour.
3. Pour into an ice cream maker and follow the manufacturer's directions.
4. Transfer to a freezer-safe container and freeze for about 4 hours, until firm.

*To make your own buttermilk, combine one cup of milk with 5 tablespoons of lemon juice and let it stand for 10 to 15 minutes before using.

Roasted Peach and Thyme Frozen Custard

Summer brings fresh, juicy peaches to market, making this the perfect summertime ice cream. And as we happen to have a peach tree in our backyard, it seemed like an obvious choice for us. Roasting the peaches at high temperature helped bring out the natural flavors. The tanginess of the thyme was a perfect accent to the sweetness of the peaches and the creaminess of the coconut milk. Adding egg yolks makes this more of a frozen custard than a true ice cream, but that just means it is extra rich and creamy!

Makes about 3½ cups custard

3 large peaches

1 tablespoon plus ¼ cup honey, divided

1 (13.5-ounce) can full-fat coconut milk

1 teaspoon pure vanilla extract

2 tablespoons roughly chopped fresh lemon thyme

2 large egg yolks

1. Preheat the oven to 400°F.
2. Cut the peaches in half, remove the pits and place the unpeeled fruit in a roasting pan, cut side up. Drizzle with 1 tablespoon of the honey and roast until soft, 30 to 40 minutes. Let cool completely and peel the skins off the peaches. Smash the peaches with a fork or potato masher—no need to puree. Cover and refrigerate.
3. In a medium-size saucepan, combine the coconut milk, the remaining ¼ cup of honey, and the vanilla and lemon thyme and bring to barely a simmer. Remove from the heat.
4. In a separate bowl, whisk the egg yolks until frothy.
5. Pour about a fourth of the hot coconut milk mixture into the egg yolks, whisking constantly. Then pour the egg yolk mixture into the remaining coconut milk mixture in the saucepan.
6. Bring the sauce to a simmer and cook, while whisking, until somewhat thickened—about 5 minutes. Remove from the heat and allow to cool for a few minutes.
7. Strain the custard through a fine sieve to remove the thyme and any lumps.
8. Refrigerate the custard until completely cooled. Alternatively, you can use an ice bath (bowl of water and ice) to cool the custard even faster before refrigerating.
9. Once they are both chilled, add the peaches to the custard base and process the ice cream according to your ice cream maker manufacturer's directions. Freeze for about 4 hours or overnight, until set.

Rum Raisin Ice Cream

My father passed away over twenty years ago, but I still remember rum raisin was his favorite kind of ice cream. My son Nathaniel takes after him in this regard. To try to faithfully re-create Dad's preferred flavor I used milk and cream, so this recipe isn't dairy free. However, it is sweetened only with raisins and maple syrup. The result is an exceptionally creamy treat that our dairy-eating son loves. I took that as a positive sign that would have made his grandfather very happy! Try it in a grain-free Waffle Cone (page 172).

Makes about 1 quart ice cream

1 cup raisins

½ cup rum

2 cups heavy whipping cream

1 cup whole, grass-fed milk

½ cup pure maple syrup

1 teaspoon pure vanilla extract

6 large egg yolks

1. Soak the raisins in the rum for about 4 hours, covered.

2. Heat the rum-soaked raisins and liquid in a medium-size pan just enough to cook out some of the alcohol but not enough to dry out the raisins. Allow it to cool completely. (If there is too much alcohol the ice cream won't harden quite as much but you could skip this step.)

3. In a medium-size saucepan, combine the cream, milk, maple syrup and vanilla and bring to barely a simmer.

4. In a separate bowl, whisk the egg yolks until frothy.

5. Pour about a fourth of the hot cream mixture into the egg yolks, whisking constantly. Pour the egg yolk mixture into the remaining cream mixture in the saucepan. Bring the sauce to a simmer and cook, while whisking, until somewhat thickened—about 5 minutes.

6. Transfer the custard to a bowl and refrigerate until cooled. Alternatively, you can use an ice bath (bowl of water and ice) to cool the custard even faster.

7. Pour the cooled custard into the bowl of an ice cream maker and process according to the manufacturer's directions. Add the rum raisins a few minutes before the end of the freezing process.

8. The ice cream will be ready to eat immediately, but if you want a harder ice cream, you can transfer to the freezer to chill for a couple of hours before serving.

Blueberry Chèvre Cheesecake Ice Cream

Chèvre is French for "goat cheese." In much of the world, goat cheese has been a dietary staple for thousands of years, but only in the last fifteen to twenty years has it become popular in the USA. So popular, in fact, that sales have been steadily climbing over the last decade, and goat cheese is now readily available in local grocery stores and supermarkets. This delicious (though not dairy-free) dessert provides the rich flavor of chèvre, the coolness of ice cream, the tanginess of fresh blueberries and the crunch of crust. It is delicious served by itself, or in Waffle Cones (page 172).

Makes about 1 quart ice cream

BLUEBERRY SAUCE

12 ounces (340 g) wild blueberries (fresh or frozen)

¼ cup raw honey

Juice of ½ lemon

BLUEBERRY CHEESECAKE ICE CREAM

8 ounces (225 g) crème fraîche

4 ounces (113 g) goat cheese

1½ cups whole milk

½ cup plus 1 tablespoon pure maple syrup

Zest of ½ lemon

1 teaspoon pure vanilla extract

¼ teaspoon finely ground sea salt

⅓ cup Almond Crumble (page 107)

1. Make the blueberry sauce: Combine the blueberries, honey and lemon juice in a medium-size saucepan. Cook over medium heat for about 5 minutes, until the blueberries soften and the juices form a syrup.

2. Transfer the blueberry sauce to a bowl and refrigerate until chilled, about 2 hours.

3. Make the ice cream: Combine the crème fraîche, goat cheese, milk, maple syrup, lemon zest, vanilla and salt in a blender and mix until smooth. Transfer to a bowl and refrigerate until fully chilled.

4. Once the blueberry sauce and ice cream base are both chilled, process the ice cream according to your ice cream maker manufacturer's directions. When it is done freezing, drain the blueberries and swirl them into the ice cream along with the almond crumble—don't overdo it or you will lose the swirl pattern.

5. Freeze until set, at least 2 hours.

Dark Chocolate Ice Cream

My children are very skeptical about coconut milk as a substitute for dairy in ice cream. I often hear, "Mom, is this REAL ice cream or is it made with coconut milk?" But in spite of the fact this rich, double chocolate ice cream has no dairy or eggs, it fooled my boys and had them coming back for seconds. The combination of coconut sugar and honey lends a brown-sugar flavor and the cocoa powder and chocolate are a one-two punch of chocolatey goodness. Adding a bit of tapioca flour serves to thicken the ice cream into a rich and creamy, truly decadent treat.

Makes about 1 quart ice cream

2 (13.5-ounce) cans full-fat coconut milk

1 tablespoon tapioca flour (optional thickener)

½ cup coconut sugar

2 tablespoons honey

⅓ cup (43 grams) unsweetened cocoa powder

2 ounces unsweetened dark chocolate, chopped

¼ teaspoon finely ground sea salt

½ teaspoon vanilla extract

1. For a thicker ice cream, make a slurry by mixing a few tablespoons coconut milk with the tapioca in a small bowl, until smooth.

2. In a medium saucepan, heat the rest of the coconut milk, coconut sugar and honey just to a boil. Turn down the heat and whisk in the cocoa powder, and let it cook at a simmer for 5 minutes.

3. Add the slurry into the ice cream mixture, then continue to cook for 1 minute, whisking constantly.

4. Remove from the heat and add the chopped chocolate, salt and vanilla and whisk until the chocolate is melted and completely incorporated.

5. Transfer the ice cream mixture to a bowl, cover and refrigerate until chilled. Alternatively, you can use an ice bath (bowl of water and ice) to chill the ice cream even faster.

6. Pour the mixture into the bowl of an ice cream maker and process according to the manufacturer's directions.

7. Transfer to the freezer for a couple of hours to harden before serving.

Cherry Swirl Coconut Frozen Custard

Frozen custard is similar to ice cream, except for the egg yolks. To qualify as custard, the mixture has to contain at least 1.4 percent egg yolk by weight, although it can contain more. The lecithin in the yolk emulsifies the mixture, giving it a rich, creamy consistency. This custard recipe was also made with fresh cherries and full-fat coconut milk instead of cream, so it's completely dairy free.

Makes about 1½ quarts custard

CHERRY SAUCE

12 ounces (340 g) pitted sweet cherries

¼ cup honey

Juice of ½ lemon

COCONUT CUSTARD

2 (13.5-ounce) cans full-fat coconut milk

½ cup raw honey

¼ cup coconut butter (optional)

Zest of 1 lemon

1 tablespoon pure vanilla extract

¼ teaspoon finely ground sea salt

4 large egg yolks

1. Make the cherry sauce: Combine the cherries, honey and lemon juice in a medium-size saucepan. Cook over medium heat for 5 to 7 minutes, until the cherries soften and the juices form a syrup.

2. Transfer the cherry sauce to a bowl and refrigerate until chilled, about 2 hours.

3. Make the coconut custard: In a medium-size saucepan, combine the coconut milk, honey, coconut butter, lemon zest, vanilla and salt and bring to barely a simmer. Remove from the heat.

4. In a separate bowl, whisk the egg yolks until frothy.

5. Pour about a fourth of the hot coconut milk mixture into the egg yolks, whisking constantly. Then pour the egg yolk mixture into the coconut milk mixture in the saucepan.

6. Bring the sauce to a simmer and cook, whisking, until somewhat thickened, about 5 minutes. Remove from the heat and allow to cool for a few minutes.

7. If you want a smoother custard, strain the mixture through a fine sieve to remove any lumps.

8. Refrigerate the custard until completely cooled. Alternatively, you can use an ice bath (bowl of water and ice) to cool the custard even faster before refrigerating.

9. Once the cherry sauce and the coconut custard are both chilled, process the custard mixture according to your ice-cream maker manufacturer's directions. When it is done freezing, drain and swirl in the cherries—don't overdo it or you will lose the swirl pattern.

10. Freeze until set, at least 2 hours.

Mixed Berry Shiraz Sorbet

T he deep, fruity taste of sorbet is another dairy-free frozen treat I learned to love while living abroad. Sorbet is typically made from sweetened water with flavoring (usually fruit, wine, or liqueur.) This recipe is an example of a combination sorbet, containing mixed berries cooked in a red Shiraz wine. The result is an intense, deep berry flavor that literally melts in your mouth. This rich sorbet goes great with a glass of sparkling mineral water.

Makes about 1 quart sorbet

3 cups blackberries plus 1 cup blueberries (or combination of favorite fresh or frozen berries)

2 cups Shiraz or similar red wine

⅓ cup honey

Mint leaves, for garnish (optional)

1. Place the berries and wine in a medium-size saucepan and bring to a simmer. Cook, covered, for 10 minutes.
2. Turn off the heat and use a wooden spoon to mash the berries to release their juices.
3. Allow to cool for 5 to 10 minutes, then use the spoon to press the mixture through a fine-mesh sieve.
4. Return the strained mixture to the pan and bring to a boil. Boil for a few minutes to cook off the alcohol and combine the flavors. Stir in the honey.
5. Cover and chill completely. Process according to your ice cream maker manufacturer's directions and serve immediately or, if you do not have an ice cream maker, simply place in your freezer as is.
6. The small amount of alcohol that remains in the sorbet will keep it from freezing completely solid, allowing it to be easily scooped into glasses or bowls.
7. Garnish with mint leaves.

Tipsy Affogato al Caffè

Desserts aren't just for kids! In fact, this sumptuous Italian dessert—often called "the Adult Sundae"—is really only meant for those of slightly more advanced years. That's because the ice cream is topped by hot, intense and highly caffeinated espresso, as well as a splash of amaretto, an Italian liqueur made primarily from almonds and apricot pits. If you tolerate dairy, you may choose to use Honey Yogurt Gelato for the base (page 155). For a dairy-free option, consider using the Basic Vanilla Bean Ice Cream (page 151). Either way, Tipsy Affogato al Caffè makes for a memorable and sophisticated, yet simple, treat any time of day.

Makes 1 serving

1 scoop (about ½ cup) Honey Yogurt Gelato, page 155 or Basic Vanilla Bean Ice Cream, page 151

1 shot (about 2 ounces [60 ml]) brewed espresso

½ ounce (15 ml) amaretto (almond liqueur)

Shaved dark chocolate or chopped nuts, for garnish (optional)

1. Place the gelato in a tumbler.
2. Pour the espresso and amaretto over the gelato.
3. Sprinkle with chocolate shavings or crushed nuts, if using. Serve immediately.

Gingerbread Men Ice Cream Sandwiches

Gingerbread Men may try to escape, even in winter, and may dress accordingly. This recipe has a somewhat arduous process but worth it for the looks on the faces of your friends or families. My kids squealed with delight upon seeing these frozen wonders, making the task more than worthwhile.

Makes 6 ice cream sandwiches

1 recipe Gingerbread Men Cookies (page 68)

Vanilla ice cream (if using Basic Vanilla Bean Ice Cream, page 151, you may need a double recipe)

1. Prepare the gingerbread men or women according to the recipe directions and let them cool completely.
2. Have ready a sheet pan that will fit flat into your freezer with a few inches' clearance.
3. Make sure your ice cream is frozen solid. If you are using ice cream from a carton, you can cut away the sides to reveal a solid block of frozen ice cream. Use a long knife to cut it into 1-inch-thick blocks on the side large enough be cut by a gingerbread man cookie cutter. Refreeze the slices on the pan until solid again.
4. Remove the ice cream slices from the freezer and quickly cut them with the cookie cutters.
5. Refreeze the cutouts on the sheet pan. Place any excess ice cream into a 9-inch square pan and mash together to form a layer that you can refreeze. Repeat the process with last remaining ice cream.
6. Use two gingerbread men cookies to sandwich the ice cream shapes. Serve immediately or wrap individually and keep in the freezer for a special treat.

Waffle Cones

Some people like ice cream in a cup or a bowl, but I like the crunchiness and flavor of a good cone. Ice cream cones first became popular in the USA during the early twentieth century after an Italian immigrant applied for and received a patent to make and sell them. Since that time, the words *ice cream* and *cone* have become practically inseparable ... and that's a good thing! These Paleo Waffle Cones can also be broken up into smaller pieces and served with your ice cream in a bowl, or as sweet, crunchy chips.

Makes 6 waffle cones

¾ cup (75 g) blanched almond flour

1 tablespoon arrowroot flour

¼ teaspoon fine finely ground sea salt

1 large egg

1 large egg white

2 tablespoons honey, or ¼ cup maple sugar

2 tablespoons liquefied coconut oil

½ teaspoon vanilla extract

1. Place all the ingredients into a high-speed blender and blend until very smooth.

2. Heat your waffle cone maker or pizzelle maker according to the manufacturer's directions.

3. Pour 1 tablespoon of batter (or more, depending on the type of waffle cone maker you are using) onto the hot waffle cone maker and cook for recommended amount of time.

4. Once the waffle is baked, follow the manufacturer's directions to roll into a cone shape. Repeat with the remaining batter.

Chocolate Bacon Almond Bark

L et that name sink in. Is there anything *not* to like about something that obviously consists of mostly chocolate . . . with almonds . . . and bacon!?!? If you like to have an occasional candy bar—heck, even if you like having one frequently—you'll enjoy this recipe. But make sure to stash it away in a safe place, because it tends to disappear fast. All natural chocolate . . . roasted almonds . . . bacon. Yes, there is something better, out there . . . we call it Heaven.

Makes about a half sheet pan's worth of bark

8 slices thick-sliced organic, free-range bacon

1 tablespoon pure maple syrup

1 cup unsalted raw or roasted almonds

¼ teaspoon (scant) finely ground sea salt

¼ teaspoon cayenne pepper or crushed red pepper flakes (optional)

16 ounces (about 450 g) dark chocolate (at least 70% dark)

1. Bake the bacon until crispy (see "Oven-Baked Bacon," page 34). Meanwhile, line a baking sheet with parchment paper or a silicone mat.

2. When the bacon is cooked, reserve 1 to 2 teaspoons of the bacon fat. Crumble the cooked bacon into a bowl along with the maple syrup, almonds, salt and pepper flakes, if using. Stir well and set aside.

3. Melt the chocolate along with the bacon fat, using a double boiler or heatproof bowl set over a saucepan of simmering water (you can also use a microwave). Slowly melt the chocolate, stirring often, until smooth. Combine the melted chocolate with the bacon mixture.

4. Pour the mixture onto the prepared baking sheet and spread out as thinly as possible.

5. Place in the refrigerator to chill until set, about 20 minutes.

6. Once set, break the bark into pieces and store in an airtight container.

Cinnamon Cheesecake Bites

Chocolate-covered, cinnamon-flavored cashew cheesecake bites are delicious and dairy-free treats. They can be frozen and wrapped individually, making them perfect when you want just a little something to take the edge off a craving for something sweet. No need to eat a large portion; just take one mini cheesecake bite out of the freezer and enjoy.

Makes 36 cheesecake bites

CHEESECAKE CRUST

1 cup (100 g) blanched almond flour

1 tablespoon (7 g) coconut flour

¼ teaspoon baking soda

⅛ teaspoon finely ground sea salt

¼ cup liquefied coconut oil, or ghee, melted

3 tablespoons pure maple syrup

1 teaspoon pure vanilla extract

CINNAMON CHEESECAKE FILLING

2 cups raw cashews, soaked for several hours or overnight, then drained and rinsed

½ cup full-fat coconut milk, apple juice, or water

½ cup pure maple syrup, or ⅓ cup raw honey

½ cup liquefied coconut oil, or ghee, melted

1 tablespoon ground cinnamon

2 teaspoons pure vanilla extract

Pinch of finely ground sea salt

1 teaspoon unflavored grass-fed gelatin or vegan equivalent (see page 27), plus 2 tablespoons warm water (optional)

CHOCOLATE COATING (OPTIONAL)

10 ounces dark chocolate, chopped

1 tablespoon coconut oil or ghee

1. Make the crust: Preheat the oven to 350°F. Prepare an 8-inch square pan by greasing it and lining with parchment paper.

2. Weigh the flours and sift together with the baking soda and salt into a medium-size bowl. Set aside.

3. Whisk together the coconut oil, maple syrup and vanilla. Add to the dry ingredients and stir until well combined.

4. Press into the bottom of the prepared pan and bake for 15 minutes. Allow to cool, then place in the freezer until ready to top with the cashew cream cheese mixture.

5. Make the filling: Place the cashews into a food processor with the coconut milk, maple syrup, coconut oil, cinnamon, vanilla and salt and carefully pulse a few times until the liquid and cashews are starting to make a paste. Stop to scrape down the sides a few times and continue to process for at least 10 minutes, until very smooth and creamy.

6. While the cashew mixture is processing, place the warm water in a small bowl, sprinkle the gelatin on top and stir until the gelatin melts completely. Immediately add it to the cashew mixture in the food processor and continue to process for another minute or two.

7. Pour the cinnamon filling over the crust. Smooth with an offset spatula. Cover with plastic wrap and place into the freezer to chill until set, at least 4 hours or overnight.

8. Once the cheesecake is set, remove the pan from the freezer, lift out the entire frozen square, and cut it into 1- to 1½-inch squares.

9. If desired, melt the chocolate and the oil, and drizzle the bites with melted chocolate or dip the squares into the chocolate to fully cover them. Place the cheesecake bites on a wire rack to set. Freeze until ready to serve.

Goat Cheese Fudge Truffles

Chocolate truffles don't contain any of the fungal delicacy so valued by devotees of haute cuisine. The name *truffle* has humble origins, and actually comes from the Latin word for "tuber," *tufera*, meaning "lumpy." Despite being definitely lumpy, these Paleo truffles, made with chèvre (goat cheese) have a lot of rich, creamy fudge flavor combined with almonds or pistachios. They can be served as an after-dinner treat with tea or coffee.

Makes 18 to 24 truffles

4 ounces goat cheese, at room temperature

10 ounces dark chocolate, melted but not too hot

¼ cup full-fat coconut milk

1 teaspoon pure vanilla extract

Pinch of finely ground sea salt

Unsweetened cocoa powder, unsweetened shredded coconut, or finely chopped pistachios or almonds, for rolling (optional)

1. Place the cheese, chocolate, coconut milk, vanilla and salt in a bowl and mix together until very smooth.

2. Place the mixture in the fridge and chill for about 10 minutes, or until the fudge is firm enough to roll into balls.

3. Use your hands to form the mixture into eighteen small, round balls; they should be half the size of a golf ball (1 to 1½ inches in diameter).

4. Roll the truffles in cocoa powder, coconut or finely chopped pistachios or almonds.

5. Place in the fridge to chill for 20 minutes before serving.

Maple Marshmallows

My younger son loves marshmallows, and could easily eat an entire bag in one sitting if I let him. He's even taken to hiding a bag of marshmallows in his sock drawer where, presumably, no one would possibly be tempted to look! This recipe was made with him in mind. I figured if he wants marshmallows, better to give him ones with all-natural ingredients. You can substitute honey for the maple syrup but only if you *really* like honey, as it imparts a very strong honey flavor. In my opinion, the maple syrup is the best option.

Makes 16 (2-inch-square) marshmallows or multiple "kisses"

3 tablespoons unflavored grass-fed gelatin or vegan equivalent (see page 27)

1 cup filtered water

1 cup pure maple syrup

¼ teaspoon finely ground sea salt

2 teaspoons pure vanilla extract

2 tablespoons tapioca flour

2 tablespoons Confectioners' sugar

1. Grease an 8-inch square baking dish; line with parchment paper with the ends hanging over two opposite sides. Sprinkle the gelatin over cup of the water in the bowl of a stand mixer; let stand for 5 minutes.

2. Heat the maple syrup, remaining ½ cup of water and the salt in a saucepan over medium-high heat, stirring occasionally, until the syrup reaches 238°F on a candy thermometer.

3. With an electric mixer fitted with the whisk attachment, whisk the gelatin on low speed, adding the syrup in a slow, steady stream down the side of the bowl. Whisk, gradually increasing the speed to high, until the mixture has almost tripled in volume, about 6 to 8 minutes. Whisk in the vanilla.

4. Transfer to the prepared pan. Smooth the top with an offset spatula. Let stand until set, at least 4 hours.

5. Once the marshmallow block is completely set, pull it out of the pan, using the parchment paper handles. Combine the tapioca and powdered sugar and dust the outside of the block of marshmallow. Cut sixteen 2-inch-square marshmallows, using a serrated knife. Coat the blade of the knife with any remaining tapioca and Confectioners' sugar mixture, as needed, to help with cutting.

ALTERNATIVE METHOD

To create marshmallow kisses, suitable for making Chocolate-Covered Marshmallow Bites (page 184), fill a pastry bag fitted with a large round or star tip, with the soft marshmallow immediately after it is done in the mixer. Pipe onto a sheet pan covered with parchment paper or a silicone mat. Allow the marshmallow kisses to set completely.

Chocolate-Covered Marshmallow Bites

Some people say smells evoke the strongest memories, but I think they're wrong. I think it's marshmallows. Admit it—what was your reaction when you read the word *marshmallow*? I'm willing to bet it was a strong one. Chances are that even now, you can visualize the puffy, spongy whiteness, feel the marshmallow in your mouth, and even taste the sugary sweetness as it dissolves, right? Now—in your mind—place it on top of a grain-free chocolate shortbread cookie and add a chocolate coating. What's your reaction this time? Exactly!

Makes about 48 bites

1 recipe Chocolate Shortbread Cookies (page 72)

1 recipe Maple Marshmallows (page 183)

10 ounces dark chocolate chips

1 teaspoon coconut oil

1. Prepare the cookies according to the recipe directions and allow them to cool completely.

2. Prepare the Maple Marshmallows and pipe into "kiss" shapes.

3. Set the cookies an inch apart on parchment paper or a wire rack. Top each cookie with one marshmallow.

4. Melt the chocolate chips with the coconut oil in a small bowl or using a double boiler, and pour over the top of a marshmallow, using just enough of the chocolate to run down and cover. Repeat to create the other Chocolate-Covered Marshmallow Bites.

5. Allow bites to cool completely. Placing them in the refrigerator will speed up the process.

Sauces and Frostings

Roasted Strawberry Sauce

One way to really bring out the natural, juicy sweetness of fresh, ripe strawberries is to roast them in the oven. This easy recipe combines the roasted strawberries and their luscious juice with raw honey, and takes less than an hour to make. If you can resist eating it all in one sitting, the remaining sauce can be refrigerated for later use. It's perfect with Crêpes (page 49) and Whipped Coconut Cream (page 205).

Makes about 1½ cups sauce

1 pound fresh, ripe strawberries (3 to 4 cups)
1 heaping tablespoon raw honey

1. Preheat the oven to 325°F.
2. Wash and drain the strawberries. Cut off the tops and then slice the berries into quarters or eighths, depending on size of the berry.
3. Cover a large sheet pan in parchment paper and spread out the strawberries in an even layer on the paper.
4. Roast, uncovered, for about 25 minutes.
5. Remove from the oven and allow to cool on the pan.
6. Place the strawberries and their juices in a bowl and stir in the raw honey.
7. Cover and chill. Will keep for at least a week in the fridge.

Simple Blackberry Sauce

Blackberries are a rich, juicy treat normally reserved for warm weather (if you want them fresh). But either fresh or frozen berries work well in this simple, syrupy sauce that combines the dark, juicy fruit with honey. Cook down to your preferred viscosity, and serve over cake, pie, ice cream or crèpes.

Makes about 1½ cups sauce

12 ounces fresh blackberries (2 to 3 cups)   Squeeze of lemon juice
4 tablespoons honey, divided

1. Place the blackberries and 2 tablespoons of the honey in a medium-size saucepan and heat over medium-high heat, stirring, for 5 to 7 minutes.
2. Use a slotted spoon to transfer the blackberries to a separate dish and reserve.
3. Add the remaining 2 tablespoons of honey to the sauce in the pan and simmer until reduced by about half, 15 to 20 minutes.
4. Add the lemon juice to the reduced sauce, pour the sauce over the reserved blackberries and stir to combine.

Avocado Chocolate Frosting

Avocado isn't just for guacamole. It's also great for chocolate frosting. Yes, that's right: chocolate frosting! One ripe avocado combined with cocoa powder and maple syrup makes a delicious, creamy frosting that's unrecognizable as avocado. Serve it to your friends, but don't tell them it's made with avocado until after they've tried it! Just enjoy their surprised expressions as they ask for seconds.

Makes enough frosting for 1 single-layer cake

1 perfectly ripe avocado, peeled and pitted

½ cup (64 g) high-quality unsweetened cocoa powder

½ cup pure maple syrup

½ teaspoon pure vanilla extract

Pinch of finely ground sea salt

¼ cup dark chocolate mini chips (optional)

1. Place the avocado flesh, cocoa powder, maple syrup, vanilla and sea salt in a food processor and mix together, stopping to scrape down the sides once or twice, until it is very smooth and creamy.

2. Stir in the chocolate chips, if using.

3. The frosting is ready to spread immediately, but you can refrigerate if you think it needs to firm up. Add a little water if it is too thick.

Spiced Caramel Sauce

Whenever my family went out for ice cream, my brother always wanted his covered in chocolate sauce. Not me. I wanted caramel. There's just something about that buttery sauce that makes everything taste extra good...at least to me! This recipe mimics that distinctive flavor without the dairy and the refined sugar. It's great drizzled on the Caramelized Banana Dessert Pizza (page 112), Pecan Praline Cheesecake (page 100) or Basic Vanilla Bean Ice Cream (page 151).

Makes about 1 cup sauce

1 (13.5-ounce) can full-fat coconut milk

¼ cup honey

¼ cup pure maple syrup

2 tablespoons ghee, unsalted pastured butter or palm shortening, melted

½ teaspoon ground cinnamon

¼ teaspoon ground ginger

Pinch of ground cloves

Pinch of finely ground sea salt

Seeds of ½ vanilla bean, pod reserved

1. Whisk together the coconut milk, honey, maple syrup, ghee, cinnamon, ginger, cloves, salt and vanilla bean seeds and place in a medium-size saucepan along with the vanilla bean pod itself.

2. Bring to a boil over medium-high heat. Watch closely so the mixture doesn't boil over and use a candy thermometer to monitor the temperature. Cook over medium-high heat, stirring often, until you reach firm-ball stage (245° to 250°F). This should take 20 to 30 minutes (or more, depending on how high your heat is).

3. Remove the pan from the heat. Remove the vanilla bean pod and stir the caramel until glossy. Pour the caramel sauce into a storage container. Keep refrigerated and reheat as necessary before serving.

TO MAKE CARAMEL CANDY

Cook to a higher temperature (260° to 270°F). Prepare a 9-inch square baking pan by greasing with coconut oil, then lining it with a layer of parchment paper with the ends coming up and over the sides. Pour the hot caramel into the prepared pan and allow it to cool completely. Lift the parchment paper out of the pan, using the parchment paper "handles," and turn out the caramel onto a cutting board. Cut caramel into your desired shape and size. Individually wrap the caramels in waxed paper.

Strawberry Cashew Cream

Vegans have long used raw cashews as a substitute for dairy. The trick is to soak the cashews in water long enough to enable a smooth, creamy result that resembles soft cheese when mixed in the food processor. This recipe combines the cashew spread with fresh strawberries and other natural ingredients to make a delicious dip for fruit or a frosting for cupcakes.

Makes about 1½ cups cashew cream

1 cup raw cashews, soaked for at least 2 hours or overnight, then drained and rinsed

1 cup sliced fresh strawberries (6 to 8 ounces)

¼ to ⅓ cup raw honey

2 tablespoons coconut oil

1 tablespoon tapioca or arrowroot flour

1½ teaspoons pure vanilla extract

1 teaspoon fresh lemon juice

⅛ teaspoon finely ground sea salt

1. Place the cashews and remaining ingredients in a food processor or high-speed blender and puree until very smooth, scraping down the sides as necessary.

2. Refrigerate for at least 1 hour.

Chocolate Hazelnut Spread

I first tried the hazelnut and chocolate spread known as Nutella when I was living in Italy, and instantly loved it. I don't eat store-bought Nutella these days because it is loaded with sugar, but I realized there's nothing in the basic ingredients truly out of bounds for Paleo eating. This recipe for homemade, Paleo chocolate hazelnut spread gets pretty close to the real thing. The texture is slightly less smooth and the flavor a tad less sweet, but to me this is a bonus, as I don't crave "sweet" as much as I used to. The finished product should be refrigerated and can be warmed prior to spreading. Just remember—this spread is *healthier* than Nutella, but it is by no means a "health food." Enjoy it in moderation, but enjoy it all the same!

Makes about 1½ cups spread

1 cup blanched hazelnuts

½ cup full-fat coconut milk

¼ cup coconut nectar, honey or pure maple syrup

¼ cup (32 g) unsweetened cocoa powder

¼ teaspoon pure vanilla extract

2 tablespoons liquefied virgin coconut oil or ghee, melted

Pinch of finely ground sea salt

1. Preheat the oven to 350°F.

2. Roast the hazelnuts on an ungreased baking sheet in the oven for 10 minutes.

3. If your hazelnuts were not already blanched, you will need to remove the skins. Once they come out of the oven, use a damp cloth to remove the skins.

4. Place the blanched hazelnuts in a food processor and puree for a few minutes, until creamy—you may have to scrape down the sides of the bowl a few times.

5. Add the coconut milk, coconut nectar, cocoa powder, vanilla, coconut oil and salt and continue to process until smooth, scraping down the sides as needed.

6. Store the spread in the refrigerator.

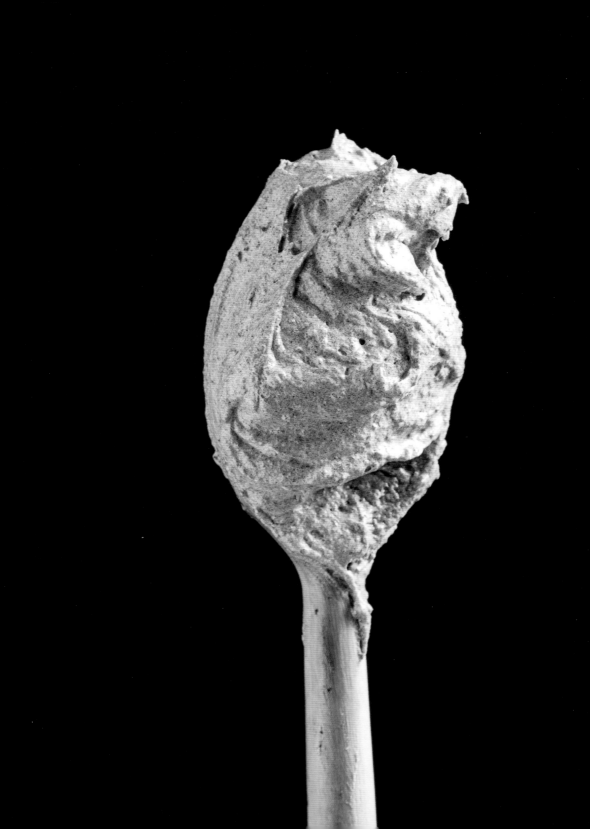

Blueberry Buttercream

This simple yet elegant frosting was made with freeze-dried blueberries. This process enables you to capture the natural flavor of the blueberries (or other fruits) without the excess moisture that fresh blueberries contain. You can use butter or substitute palm shortening to create a dairy-free, vegan-friendly topping for cakes and cupcakes.

Makes enough to frost a single-layer cake or 12 cupcakes

1.5 ounces (42 g) freeze-dried blueberries (do not use dehydrated or dried fruit)

1 cup (2 sticks) unsalted, grass-fed butter or palm shortening, at room temperature

½ cup coconut sugar

Pinch of finely ground sea salt

1. Place the blueberries in a food processor or high-speed blender and process to a fine powder. For best results, use a coffee grinder to get the particles as small as possible. Use a fine sieve or strainer to sift the pulverized freeze-dried fruit to remove any large pieces or seeds. Reprocess the larger pieces for more fruit powder.

2. In the bowl of a stand mixer, place the butter, coconut sugar and pinch of salt. Cream together until smooth. Add the powdered freeze-dried blueberries and mix until a fluffy frosting forms, about 5 minutes. You will need to scrape down the sides several times to ensure even mixing.

TO FROST CUPCAKES

Fit a frosting bag with a 9 mm star tip and fill the bag with the frosting. Starting about 1 cm away from the edge of a cupcake, pump out the frosting and continue in a spiral until you reach the center. Repeat until you have frosted all the cupcakes.

NOTE: Use more freeze-dried fruit for even more dramatic color and flavor (see photo of Almond Flour Vanilla Cupcakes, page 94). The frosting will retain a somewhat gritty texture, depending on how finely the blueberries are pulverized. If your coconut sugar is moist, it should mix well with the butter or shortening. If it is drier and more granulated, try pulverizing it in a food processor or coffee grinder for a smoother end product.

Maple Cashew Glaze

This sweet, delicious glaze is terrific as a topping for cake, cookies, donuts or even ice cream. It's made from raw cashew cream, a vegan specialty often used as a stand-in for cheese, sweetened with organic maple syrup and coconut butter. This glaze is wonderful on the Spiced Harvest Cake (page 102)—the maple flavor is the perfect complement to the spices in the cake and so delicious you will not miss cream cheese frosting.

Makes about 1 cup frosting

½ cup raw cashews, soaked for at least 2 hours or overnight, then drained and rinsed

¼ cup coconut butter, heated

¼ cup pure maple syrup

2 tablespoons liquefied coconut oil

Pinch of finely ground sea salt

Filtered water

1. Place the cashews along with the coconut butter, maple syrup, coconut oil and salt in a food processor or high-speed blender and process until smooth and creamy (this will take several minutes), scraping down the sides as necessary.

2. Add a tablespoon of filtered water at a time until you reach your desired consistency for either frosting or glazing.

Whipped Coconut Cream

Whipped coconut cream is not some sad alternative for those of us who are dairy free and cannot have the real thing. This stuff is amazingly delicious and every bit as rich and decadent as regular dairy whipped cream. You will not feel deprived in any way and the options for use are seemingly endless. I like to use whipped coconut cream as a topping for desserts or to lighten fancy sauces, such as the Champagne Sabayon (page 213). A dollop or two over a simple bowl of fruit or on a stack of pancakes is perfect even without any added sweetener. If you will be serving the whipped coconut cream immediately, there is no real need to add a stabilizer. However, if you would like a firmer whipped cream that can withstand sitting at room temperature for a bit of time, you may want to check out the Stabilized Whipped Coconut Cream (page 206).

Makes about 1 cup whipped cream

1 (13.5-ounce) can full-fat coconut milk (see note)

1 tablespoon raw honey or pure maple syrup, or to taste (optional)

1 teaspoon pure vanilla extract (optional)

1. Place the can of coconut milk in the refrigerator and leave it there until well chilled, preferably overnight.
2. Open the can and scoop out the firm layer of coconut cream that has solidified at the top. (Use only the solid cream, not the coconut water at the bottom of the can. You can use the coconut water for smoothies, such as the Easy Strawberry Banana Milkshake, page 54.)
3. Place this solid cream in the bowl of a stand mixer or a large bowl. (Chilling the bowl beforehand is recommended.)
4. In a stand mixer fitted with the whisk attachment, or a hand mixer, whip the coconut cream on high speed until it becomes fluffy and light, with soft peaks; this will take just a minute or two.
5. Mix in the honey and vanilla, if using.
6. Serve immediately or store in a sealed container in the refrigerator for up to a week. Rewhip the cream prior to serving.

NOTE: Light coconut milk will *not* work for this recipe. You may also occasionally come across a full-fat can that does not separate or have enough fat. Native Forest is a brand I have used with good success, but you can sometimes find cans of coconut cream (*not* the same as creamed coconut or cream of coconut; see "Coconut Products," page 11) in stores. You can also order coconut cream online.

Stabilized Whipped Coconut Cream

Even dairy whipped cream does not keep well for long periods of time out of the refrigerator. This is especially true with whipped coconut cream, which needs to stay cold to retain its form. By whipping bloomed gelatin into the whipped coconut cream, you will have a more stable end product that will hold up for longer periods of time.

Makes 1 to 1½ cups whipped cream

1 teaspoon unflavored grass-fed gelatin or vegan
  equivalent (see page 27)

4 teaspoons cold water

1 cup very cold coconut cream

1 to 2 tablespoons raw honey

1 teaspoon pure vanilla extract (optional)

1. In a small pan, sprinkle the gelatin into the cold water; let stand until thick. (Alternatively, place the water in a small ramekin, sprinkle with the gelatin, let stand until thick then heat in the microwave on high for no more than 10 seconds.)

2. While the gelatin is blooming, in a stand mixer fitted with a whisk attachment or using a hand mixer, whip the cold coconut cream with the raw honey until combined and smooth.

3. Heat the blooming gelatin over low heat, stirring constantly, just until the gelatin dissolves. Remove from the heat and allow to cool but not to set.

4. While continuing to beat, slowly add the liquefied gelatin to the coconut cream mixture. Add the vanilla, if using.

5. Whip at high speed until thickened.

Chocolate Ganache and Bacon Frosting

In my humble opinion, dark chocolate and crunchy bacon go great together. It's salty, sweet and crunchy, like chocolate-covered pretzels. I can't eat pretzels, but I can—and do—eat bacon. You can make this chocolate ganache frosting and leave out the bacon, if you prefer…but I wouldn't recommend it!

Makes about 1 cup frosting

8 ounces dark chocolate (preferably 100% dark/ bittersweet baking chocolate)

2 tablespoons coconut oil

4 to 6 tablespoons pure maple syrup

4 pieces crisp cooked bacon (see "Oven-Baked Bacon," page 34), chopped into bits (optional)

1. Chop the chocolate into small pieces and place in a double boiler or a heatproof bowl on top of a pot of water and bring to a simmer.
2. As the chocolate begins to melt, add the coconut oil and maple syrup.
3. Stir gently until the mixture melts and is smooth.
4. Check the taste and add a little more maple syrup, if you prefer.
5. Allow the chocolate ganache to cool.
6. Stir in the bacon pieces, if using.

Italian Meringue Buttercream

I have never been a huge fan of standard frosting. In the past I almost always asked for a middle piece of sheet cake at a birthday party because it has less frosting than the edge pieces. The exception is Italian Meringue Buttercream. This smooth and silky frosting uses egg whites combined with butter for a light and airy, very spreadable and stable frosting. Using butter is classic but I have also made this frosting with palm shortening, which is a great alternative for those who prefer to remain dairy free.

Makes about 3 cups meringue buttercream, enough to frost a two-layer cake

3 large egg whites, at room temperature

½ teaspoon cream of tartar

⅛ teaspoon finely ground sea salt

½ cup honey or pure maple syrup

1½ cups (3 sticks) unsalted pastured butter or palm shortening, at room temperature,

2 teaspoons pure vanilla extract

1. Place the egg whites in the bowl of a stand mixer. Make sure it is completely clean and free of any fat residue or else the egg whites will not whip properly.

2. Using an electric mixer fitted with the whisk attachment, begin whipping the eggs on medium speed until they are frothy and just starting to whip. Stop and sprinkle in the cream of tartar and sea salt. Start mixing again and gradually increase the speed until you have reached the firm peaks stage.

3. Heat the honey to almost boiling—either on the stovetop or in the microwave on high. With the mixer still running on medium-high speed, gradually pour in the hot honey. This will heat the meringue and pasteurize the egg whites. Continue processing for about 10 more minutes, until the meringue is cool.

4. With the mixer still running, begin adding the butter about 1 tablespoon at a time, until fully incorporated. The meringue will deflate significantly. Add the vanilla and continue to process until the frosting comes back together and enough air is whipped back in to create a light and fluffy frosting, 5 to 10 minutes. If the frosting does not whip properly even after several minutes, try refrigerating it for a few minutes, until the fat firms up. Whip again for a fluffy result.

NOTE: Vanilla is the classic choice for Italian Meringue Buttercream, but there are myriad ways to transform this basic recipe. Try adding cocoa powder or espresso powder or even pulverized freeze-dried fruit powder (see the process described in the Blueberry Buttercream, page 201) for different flavor options.

Honey Coconut Frosting

If you love light and fluffy frostings but do not have the time or inclination to make Italian Meringue Buttercream—or do not consume eggs—this recipe is for you. The palm shortening is combined with rich coconut cream and natural honey, then whipped until you achieve a cloudlike result. Use a vegan honey substitute for a vegan version.

Makes about 2½ cups frosting, enough to frost 1 (5-inch) two-layer cake

1 cup cold-pressed palm shortening

¾ cup coconut cream

⅓ cup raw honey or vegan honey substitute

¼ teaspoon pure vanilla extract

1. Combine all the ingredients in the bowl of a stand mixer and, using the whisk attachment, beat on low speed for about 30 seconds. Scrape down the sides of the bowl and continue to beat on high until the frosting is fluffy and thickened. The frosting will "break" when you first start mixing it. Just keep going (don't give up!) and it will eventually come back together and be light and fluffy like whipped cream, about 10 minutes.

2. Store the frosting in the refrigerator if you will not be consuming it immediately. Rewhip as necessary.

Champagne Sabayon

Sabayon is known as *zabaglione* in Italian. I fondly remember eating zabaglione-flavored gelato while strolling through scenic towns in Italy many years ago. I always wanted to try making the sauce myself but assumed it was too difficult and not worth the time and effort. It turns out making sabayon is not nearly as complicated I first thought. Once you get the technique down, it will be easy to impress friends and family with this sophisticated, exquisite sauce. The use of Champagne brings the sabayon up a notch but any type of sparkling fruit juice will be fine. You will enjoy the interplay of carbonation bubbles with the custard sauce and lightness of the addition of Whipped Coconut Cream (page 205). It is perfect when served simply over fresh fruit.

Makes about 3 cups sauce

6 large egg yolks

⅓ cup honey

⅔ cup (165 ml) Champagne or sparkling clear fruit juice

1 cup (250 ml) Whipped Coconut Cream without honey or maple syrup, (page 205)

1. By hand with a whisk or in a stand mixer fitted with the whisk attachment, on low speed, whisk the eggs yolks, honey, and Champagne until frothy, about 1 minute. Place the bowl over a pot partly filled with simmering water (do not let the bottom of the mixing bowl touch the boiling water). Hand whisk the sabayon until it thickens, about 3 minutes.

2. Immediately transfer the bowl to the mixer and whip the sabayon on medium-high speed until the bowl feels cool to the touch and the sabayon is pale and thick.

3. Fold the Whipped Coconut Cream into the cooled sabayon.

4. Serve immediately over fresh fruit or as part of a verrine, such as in the Champagne Sabayon and Almond Crumble Verrines (page 132).

Simple Chocolate Sauce

Simple chocolate sauce should be, well, simple. Melt some high-quality dark chocolate with the liquid of your choice, sweeten it (or not!) to your taste and make it thinner or thicker by adding liquid or chocolate.

Makes about ¾ cup sauce

6 ounces 70% cacao dark chocolate, coarsely chopped

¼ cup full-fat coconut milk or water, plus more as needed

1 tablespoon honey or pure maple syrup, or to taste

1. Melt the chocolate with the coconut milk and honey in a small saucepan over low heat (or use a double boiler). Stir constantly, without letting the mixture simmer or boil, until all the ingredients are melted and the sauce is smooth. Add additional coconut milk, as needed, to adjust the consistency of the sauce. Adjust the amount of honey to your taste.

2. Serve over ice cream, cake or fruit. This simple chocolate sauce can be stored covered in the refrigerator for about 2 weeks. Reheat in the microwave or in a heatproof bowl set directly in a pan of barely simmering water.

Acknowledgments

Gratitude and love to all who helped make this book possible:

To my husband and best friend, Gavin. Thank you for all the research and writing, for playing sous chef, for hopping in the car and picking up ingredients at a moment's notice. You tolerated my stress, helped me through my many dilemmas and never shrank from cleaning the kitchen so I could focus on creating recipes. I could not have done this without you. I love you.

To my mom, Louise Hendry Womack. You are the most amazing artist. I could only hope to have a fraction of your talent. Collaborating with you on photography was so much fun even at such a long distance. What would we do without technology?! Thanks for all your support and for being such an important part of this project.

To my sons, Benjamin and Nathaniel. Thank you for being my food testing subjects and models and for all your (very) honest opinions. I wish I could promise to stop taking so many photos of you and of food but that is probably not going to happen. Sorry! You are the lights of my life and the reasons for the spring in my steps.

To Jonah Kleitsch, my most enthusiastic taste-tester and reliable source of positive feedback. You are welcome at our house any time.

To my brothers and sisters at Garretson Road Church of Christ for all your loving support and willingness to give some of my most ambitious recipes a try.

To Kermit Hummel and Lisa Sacks for having faith in my abilities. Best wishes in your exciting new endeavors. To Ann Treistman for going to bat for me on a new vision for this book. And to Sarah Bennett for all your hard work and for tolerating my perfectionism.

Special thanks to Joan Loree of Country Antiques in Pluckemin, NJ and to Pamela Lance, and Dan and MJ Zachary for generously lending some gorgeous food photography props.

"Friendship is unnecessary, like philosophy, like art...
It has no survival value; rather it is one of those things which give value to survival."
-C.S. Lewis

Allergy-Friendly Recipes

EGG-FREE RECIPES

Flax Eggs (26)

Chia Seed Egg Substitute (26)

Almond Flour/Meal (32)

Oven-Baked Bacon (34)

Homemade Nut Milk (36)

Homemade Coconut Milk (37)

Homemade Ghee (38)

Coconut Butter Icing (46)

Crystallized Ginger Scones (53)

Easy Strawberry Banana Milkshake (54)

Paleo Granola (58)

Paleo Breakfast Porridge (61)

Best Ever Chocolate Chip Cookies (67)

Gingerbread Men Cookies (68)

Chocolate Shortbread Cookies (72)

Double Chocolate Pistachio Biscotti (84)

Pecan Praline Cheesecake (100)

Almond Crumble (107)

Coconut Milk Panna Cotta (131)

Mexican Chocolate Mousse (135)

Grilled Apricots with Honeyed Almonds and
Coconut Cream (147)

Basic Vanilla Bean Ice Cream (151)

Pistachio Ice Cream (152)

Honey Yogurt Gelato (155)

Blueberry Chèvre Cheesecake Ice Cream (160)

Dark Chocolate Ice Cream (163)

Mixed Berry Shiraz Sorbet (167)

Tipsy Affogato al Caffè (168)

Gingerbread Men Ice Cream Sandwiches (171)

Chocolate Bacon Almond Bark (177)

Cinnamon Cheesecake Bites (178)

Goat Cheese Fudge Truffles (180)

Maple Marshmallows (183)

Chocolate-Covered Marshmallow Bites (184)

Roasted Strawberry Sauce (189)

Simple Blackberry Sauce (190)

Avocado Chocolate Frosting (193)

Spiced Caramel Sauce (194)

Strawberry Cashew Cream (197)

Chocolate Hazelnut Spread (198)

Blueberry Buttercream (201)

Maple Cashew Glaze (202)

Whipped Coconut Cream (205)

Stabilized Whipped Coconut Cream (206)

Chocolate Ganache and Bacon Frosting (207)

Honey Coconut Frosting (210)

Simple Chocolate Sauce (214)

NUT-FREE RECIPES

Flax Eggs (26)

Chia Seed Egg Substitute (26)

Meringue (31)

Oven-Baked Bacon (34)

Homemade Coconut Milk (37)

Homemade Ghee (38)

Coconut Butter Icing (46)

Crèpes (49)

Cherry Clafoutis (50)

Easy Strawberry Banana Milkshake (54)

Fluffy Coconut Flour Pancakes (57)

Vanilla Madeleines (75)

Chocolate Madeleines (76)

Raspberry Coconut Macaroons (79)

Paleo Chocolate Birthday Cake (89)

Chocolate Beet Pudding Cake (90)

Angel Food Cake (96)

Apple Cider Donuts (99)

Spiced Harvest Cake (102)

Chocolate Macaroon Crust (116)

Dessert Pizza Crust (127)

Coconut Milk Panna Cotta (131)

Mexican Chocolate Mousse (135)

Pastry Cream (136)

Meyer Lemon Curd (139)

Crème Brûlée (140)

Tiramisu (143)

Honey Yogurt Gelato (155)

Roasted Peach and Thyme Frozen Custard (156)

Rum Raisin Ice Cream (159)

Dark Chocolate Ice Cream (163)

Cherry Swirl Coconut Frozen Custard (164)

Mixed Berry Shiraz Sorbet (167)

Goat Cheese Fudge Truffles (180)

Maple Marshmallows (183)

Roasted Strawberry Sauce (189)

Simple Blackberry Sauce (190)

Avocado Chocolate Frosting (193)

Spiced Caramel Sauce (194)

Blueberry Buttercream (201)

Whipped Coconut Cream (205)

Stabilized Whipped Coconut Cream (206)

Chocolate Ganache and Bacon Frosting (207)

Italian Meringue Buttercream (209)

Honey Coconut Frosting (210)

Champagne Sabayon (213)

Simple Chocolate Sauce (214)

ALL RECIPES ARE DAIRY-FREE OR HAVE A DAIRY-FREE OPTION EXCEPT THE FOLLOWING:

Honey Yogurt Gelato (155)

Rum Raisin Ice Cream (159)

Blueberry Chèvre Cheesecake Ice Cream (160)

Goat Cheese Fudge Truffles (180)

Index